# SPRING COMES TO CHICAGO

## ALSO BY CAMPELL McGRATH

*Capitalism*
*American Noise*
*Road Atlas*
*Florida Poems*

# SPRING COMES
# TO CHICAGO

## CAMPBELL MCGRATH

**ecco**

An Imprint of HarperCollinsPublishers

HarperCollins books may be purchased for educational, business, or sales
promotional use. For information, please e-mail the Special Markets Department at
SPsales@harpercollins.com.

*Acknowledgements*
"The First Trimester" appeared originally in *Antaeus.*
"The Secret Life of Capital" and "The Triumph of Rationalism" appeared in *TriQuarterly.*
"The Golden Angel Pancake House" appeared in *Third Coast.*
"Spring Comes to Chicago" appeared in *The Ohio Review.*

I would like to thank the Illinois Arts Council for a grant which helped in the completion of this
book.

I would like to thank Cathy Bowman, Jim Chandler, Bruce Craven and Reginald Gibbons for
their help over the nine-year gestation of "The Bob Hope Poem"; without their advice and
encouragement this book would have been consigned to the limbo of the stillborn, and its author
reduced to gibbering insanity.

Library of Congress Cataloging-in-Publication Data

McGrath, Campbell, 1962-
Spring comes to Chicago / Campbell McGrath.—1st ed.
p.    cm.
I. Title
PS3563.C3658S67   1996
811'.54—dc20        96-17162

Designed by Fearn Cutler de Vicq de Cumptich
The text of this book is set in Granjon

15 ❖/RRD 10 9

FIRST EDITION

For Elizabeth: *ad absurdum*.

For Sam: *ex utero*.

# CONTENTS

# SPRING COMES TO CHICAGO

# PART I

# JOY

# THE GOLDEN ANGEL PANCAKE HOUSE

Or coming out of Bento on a wild midwinter
midnight, or later, closing time Ron says, the last
rack of pool balls ratcheted down until dawn,
bottles corked and watered, lights out, going out
the door beneath the El tracks over Clark and Sheffield,
always a train showing up just then, loud, sure
as hell showering sparks upon the snowfall,
shaking slightly the lights and trestles, us
in our fellowship shouting and scurrying
like the more sprightly selves we once inhabited
behind parked cars and street signs, thinking,
hey, should we toss some snowballs? Bull's eye,
the beauty of fresh snow in the hands, like rubbing
tree-bark to catch that contact high direct
from the inexplicable source, unique however
often repeated, carried along on woolen thumbs
to the next absolutely necessary thing,
sloe gin fizzes to Green Mill jazz or the horror
of Jägermeister at the Ginger Man or
one of those German bars up around Irving Park
where a sup of the Weiss beer on tap is enough
to convince me to foreswear my stake in any vision
of the afterlife you might care to construct, say
the one with the photo of the owner in his Nazi
uniform beside a pristine fjord, could be Norway,
1940? Whichever, we're hungry now, cast out
into the false dawn of snow-coiffed streetlights
embowed like bowl-cut adolescents or
Roman emperors sated on frost, thumbs up
or down to hash & eggs at Manny's
or the locally infamous Alps, then there's one
at which I never ate though it looked absolutely
irreplaceable, the Golden Angel Pancake House,
which is a poem by Rilke I've never read
though I've used its restroom, seen its dim
celestial figures like alien life-forms
in a goldfish bowl, tasted its lonely nectar
in every stack of silver dollar buttermilk flapjacks,
though the food, for all I know, is unutterably
awful, the way it resonates is what carries me

down the swirled chords of memory
toward the bottom of the frosted glass
aquarium of dreams, whatever that means, it's
what it meant to me coming home those nights
from the Lutheran college after teaching
the *Duino Elegies* to the daughters and sons
of Minnesota farmers, the footbridge over
the North Branch of the Chicago River, frozen
solid, eddies of whirling ionized powder
around my boots in the bone-cold subzero
that makes the lights in the windows of houses
so painfully beautiful—is it the longing
to get the hell inside or the tears the wind
inevitably summons forth? Homeward,
all the way down Lincoln Avenue's amazing
arabesques and ethnic configurations
of Korean babushkas and Croatian karaoke
that feeling set upon me like the overture to god
knows what dread disease, that cathartic, lustral,
yes, idiot laughter, threat of tears in the gullet,
adam's apple stringing its yoyo to follow
the bouncing ball, as if boulevards of such purity
could countenance no science but eudaemonics,
hardly likely, as if this promethean eruption
were merely one of the more colorful dog-
and-pony acts of simple happiness, acrobatic
dromedaries or narcoleptic dancing bears,
but which I've come to see with perfect hindsight
was no less than the mighty strongman
joy himself bending bars of steel upon a tattooed
skull, so much nobler and more rapacious
than his country cousins, bliss, elation, glee,
a troupe of toothless, dipsomaniacal clowns,
multiform and variable as flurries from blizzards,
while joy is singular, present tense, predatory, priapic,
paradoxically composed of sorrow and terror
as ice is made of water, dense and pure,
darkly bejewelled, music rather than poetry,
preliterate, lapidary, dumb as an ox, cruel as youth,
magnificent and remorseless as Chicago in winter.

# PART 2

# THE
# BOB HOPE POEM

# I

## THE SECRET LIFE OF CAPITAL

*It is a great temptation to try to make the spirit explicit.*
                                                    —*Wittgenstein*

These elephantine snowflakes sashaying lazily earthward look about as
        likely as three-dollar bills.
Huge and shambling, avuncular as church-goers, delicately laced as linen
        doilies, fluffy as kittens or cotton swabs,
linked arm in arm in a ticker-tape parade of paper doll Rockettes or
        lurching like waves of drunken longshoremen

they're larger than life,
bigger than medicine balls,

they're just about as plump and juicy as the pork chops at the
        unpronounceable Polish restaurant on Milwaukee Avenue,

yes, double-stuffed—
hallelujah,
it's raining T-bones,

it's snowing Birdseye frozen vegetables, a succotash blizzard of sweet baby
        limas and tender corn niblets,

such terms of endearment, such love,

thank you, thank you,
Madison Avenue.

Now a flake has become ensnared in an invisible eddy or gyre of air outside
        my window and circles and circles
the way the liners must be up there, above the iron clouds, waiting for the
        runways at O'Hare to clear.

Which my sidewalk surely isn't.

◆

I wonder where
that old snow shovel
went?

◆

Didn't I see something like this in the movie *Airport*?

Dean Martin copiloting a disaster-prone jumbo jet jam-packed with
      memorable cameos and extras,
while Burt Lancaster and George Kennedy scramble to clear the
      snowbound, ice-riven, terror-stricken tarmac?

How many planes do you suppose are up there today?
Have they got fuel or altitude to reach the blue above this front?
How high does such a system ascend?

I guess the passengers must have read the in-flight magazine several dozen
      times by now.

I've been reading about Bob Hope in *People* magazine.
It's my wife who buys it.
I swear.

Though I have been known to cast a glance,
a quick perusal, a tiny peek
or two, it's true.

No.
Let's be perfectly
frank.

The truth is I've been sitting here for over an hour, feet on the desk, chair
      tilted back, drinking black currant tea and reading *People*
while the ubiquitous squirrels frolic and dance and the snowflakes do their
      gravitational thing.

I wanted it,
I longed for it,
I craved its guilty familiarity,

saucy headline like a hooker's smooch upon a satin lapel.

I searched the house to find it,

buried by papers and take-out menus from Ho Wah Garden, and brought it
     here, carried it right to the desk—
but no, I didn't even dare to pick it up, couldn't find the courage to carry it,
     but merely slid it across the floor with my foot,
as if I could mitigate my guilt so easily, as if I could deny any act of will or
     intention and simply discover its fortuitous presence

there, on the rug, by my chair.

Well, well, well.
*People* magazine.
Guess I'll take a look.

How sad. How banal. How pitiful
our interests,
simple or compounded daily.

How profligate to grant unthinking assent to this most glib and hour-
     wasting gratification, though time, as they say, is money,

and times are tough,
and money does not grow on trees,
and nothing makes money like money.

&#9670;


   Money, said the seven sages of Greece, is the blood and soul of men and
   he who has none wanders dead among the living.
                                   —Scipio de Gramont, *Le Dernier Royal*


&#9670;


They say in this issue of *People* that Bob Hope is in a hot dispute about a
     piece of real estate in Southern California.
As he likes to joke with Jay on Johnny he owns at least half of everything
     left out there,
the yucca flats and salt pans beyond Antelope Valley, the chaparral and
     scrub oak of the Santa Monica Mountains,

dry hills and canyons so far out it must have seemed nuts to imagine the city
    could ever reach them.
But now it has, and it's his, and he wants a championship golf course and
    hundreds of beautiful ranch-style homes
to replace this particular oasis above the smog line, he likes developers more
    than conservationists,
doesn't understand the theory, really, old school, rights of property, it's his
    and he'll do what he likes,
so what if he's a nonagenarian he wants that extra twenty-five million bucks
    so bad he can taste it.

There are those who cannot comprehend this line of reasoning.

What does he want with more millions, such a rich and ancient man?
What's driven him to this desire for money beyond all rational definition of
    need?
What does he think it can buy that he doesn't already have?

What is it with this generation of white men from Southern California, the
    oil barons and water hoarders,
the highway builders, the golf players, the dream merchants and the
    oligarchs and the last frontiersmen,
Uncle Walt and the Duke, Nixon's Committee of 100 and the whole
    Reagan crew,
who willingly testified to their fondness for none but former Marines and
    self-made millionaires like themselves?

They are such fossils!
I mean that constructively.

Is not the very earth we stand upon built from the bones of the past?

Are not these men somehow akin to the animate saber-rattling skeletons of
    a Saturday morning Sinbad movie,
synecdochical cenotaphs of war and hegemony, of the Great Depression and
    the Pax Americana,
a golden age of capital acquisition when the romance of wealth glowed like
    some uncharted Polynesian atoll awaiting initial contact,

though they say
no man is an island,

and I assume that these of all men would deny the implicitly pro-union
    metaphor of sedimentation,
preferring instead the heroic agency of individual enactment, the volcanic
    will that lifted the Hawaiian archipelago from the deep Pacific abyss,
which indeed is one of the two viable geological models for island-
    building—the other being the slow communal accretion of coral.


    ♦


Beyond the priestly class, and ranged in an ascending hierarchy, ordi-
narily comes a superhuman vicarious leisure class of saints, angels,
etc.—or their equivalents in the ethnic cults. These rise in grade, one
above another, according to an elaborate system of status. The principle
of status runs through the entire hierarchical system, both visible and
invisible.

—Thorstein Veblen, Theory of the Leisure Class


    ♦


Two sums of money are distinguishable only by their amount.

—Marx, Das Kapital


    ♦


The thing that really gets me about Bob is, there should be no magical aura
    or mystical signification attached to money.
A house, a car, a pool, a mountain, a harem, an empire: it buys a lot, but
    nothing you don't know about.
There is no phantom realm: fat cats eat club sandwiches and drink iced tea
    after eighteen holes just like you do.
So maybe they had pheasant last night and you had Dinty Moore, does it
    really matter?
I honestly believe that Dinty Moore tastes better, which is beside the point, I
    admit, but who says we can't engage in a little sophistry

in pursuit of our ideals?

Sure, money's more powerful than neutron bombs,

it is the lever of Archimedes,
it is the rainbow

but not the pot of gold.

It's a beautiful metaphor, a poetic analogy,

a diagram,
a model,
a map of the stars,

doppelganger, robot, tool, system, language, operating software for the
    super computer of western civilization.

It is a means to an end, and to make of it an end in itself is the worst kind of
    semantic confusion,
mistaking the mechanics of an imperfect system for the values that system
    seeks to descibe,
like mastering the laws of astrophysics without stopping to look at the stars,
    like memorizing road maps before learning to drive a car.

It is
what it is
and it is what it is

n't,

the veil through which we glimpse the workings of the great machine,
the shadow that knows which evil lurks in the fondest heart,
the green- or rose-colored lens before our eyes.

◆

Like ocean navigation or printing, money and credit are techniques,
which can be reproduced and perpetuated. They make up a single lan-
guage, which every society speaks after its fashion, and which every in-
dividual is obliged to learn.
                                        —Fernand Braudel, *Civilization & Capitalism*

◆

Money talks.

It coughs, cries, whispers, screams, wheedles, boasts, exhorts,

it is Doolittle's polyglot
and the fall of the Tower of Babel,

a mirror,
a flag,
a signal fire

in the smoke of whose burning we live out our lives.

Mesopotamian barley and the cattle of the Visigoths,
the milling of corn and steel and wood pulp,
wampum, feathers, cowrie shells, dogs' teeth,

T-bills, junk bonds, derivatives, munis, arbs and strips,
salt, tobacco, leather, pigs, nails, ingots, bullion,
the ceremonial stone wheels of the lost empire of Yap,

Rockefeller's lucky nickels and Bill Gates' paper billions,
crude oil into gasoline, raw molasses into rum,
the Arabs from whom we borrowed the zeros of our millions

and the Lydians minting gold beneath Croesus' thumb,
silk merchants of Venice, the credit banks of Genoa,
heavy-laden slave ships bound for Charleston, Havana, Belém,

schillings, shekels, rubles, rupees, dinars, escudos, drachma,
yen, sen, won, kips, leks, birrs, dongs, sylis, kyats, takas, kwanzas,
ringgits, tugriks, quetzals, ngultrums, bolivars, balboas,

moolah,
jack,
simoleons and mazuma:

it all amounts to the same thing,
which is everything
or nothing,

depending on where you stand.

Location, location, location,
as they say
in the real estate biz.

◆

At a certain season of our life we are accustomed to consider every spot as the possible site of a house. I have thus surveyed the country on every side within a dozen miles of where I live. In imagination I have bought all the farms in succession, for all were to be bought, and I knew their price. I walked over each farmer's premises, tasted his wild apples, discoursed on husbandry with him, took his farm at his price, mortgaging it to him in my mind; even put a higher price on it,—took everything but a deed of it,—took his word for his deed, for I dearly love to talk,—cultivated it, and him too to some extent, I trust, and withdrew when I had enjoyed it long enough, leaving him to carry on. This experience entitled me to be regarded as a sort of real-estate broker by my friends.

—Thoreau, *Walden*

◆

So you see, we're not blind to that blissful allure.

We too have tasted those wild apples,
we too have taken word for deed,

though not without a title search, termite inspection, and an additional
three-and-a-half points up front.

Land speculation
is a national fixation!

From the thirteen colonies to the three-millionth subdivision, William Penn
to William Levitt, Benjamin Franklin to Donald Trump.
It was Jefferson himself who laid the grid for the national survey, the great
lineation, the mighty matrix,
the checkerboard plat in which we are stuck like squared-off sardines in
kindergarten cubbyholes
or freight containers stacked in a drafty warehouse, any one of which could
be full of cash, if the price is right,
though most contain shipments of knock-off athletic shoes, plastic combs or
fuzzy troll pencil eraser toys manufactured in Hong Kong.

Who can tell, from this distance, just where to place their bet?
Which meridian to mortgage, which cubby to corner?

Which special seminar to master the arcane science of squeezing profit from
    land with no money down as seen on late-night cable TV?


    &#9670;


Not that it's an easy trick to bear in mind the object lessons of Dave Del
    Dotto or commodity fetishism
when bombarded by America's insistent visions of dancing sugar plums and
    juicy starlets' implanted breasts in *People* magazine,
when "Lifestyles of the Rich and Famous" demeans you daily with
    exclusive tidbits from the latest tropical fantasy retreat,

the hippest high desert mineral-mud spa,
the in, the with-it, the p.c., the now.

Who can keep the jargon straight?

It's like these academic journals my friend David sends me from Berkeley,
    *Social Inquest, Contemporary Amazonia, The Bulletin of Marxist*
    *Heuristics.*

Here's a totemistic reconsideration of Franz Boas among the Kwakiutl,
    bear and salmon, eagle and orca,
the potlatch as a model of economic reversal akin to the Toka ceremony of
    Western Melanesia.
Here's an investigation into the spiritual subjunction of the legendarily
    ferocious Munducuru,
disarmed not by strength or guile of the soldiers and missionaries crawling
    up the brown river fingers of the Amazon hand,

but by salt, manioc flour, cotton,
iron and sugar and rice.

Here's an analysis of the magico-religious peasant culture of the Cauca
    Valley in Colombia,
where mystification at the essential life force of money has led to *el bautizo*
    *del billete,* the illegal baptism of peso notes,
to make their capital fruitful, lucky, blessed, so that it will return, like a
    homing pigeon,
trailing flocks of fellow bills as literal interest, flights of animate currency in
    the wake of the sanctified rainmaker.

One of the few successful black store owners in the village was saved from a great loss only by a most unusual coincidence. Serving in his shop he was startled to hear a strange noise in his cash register. Peering in he saw two bills fighting with each other for possession of the contents, and he realized that two customers, each with their own baptized bills, must have just paid them over and were awaiting their return. This strange coincidence allowed him to prevent the spiriting away of his cash.

—Michael Taussig, "The Genesis of Capitalism Amongst a South American Peasantry: Devil's Labor and the Baptism of Money"

♦

Of course I do get other kinds of mail.
It isn't all from Berkeley.

For Christmas my brother's girlfriend sent me an autographed eight-by-ten
        glossy of Kenny Rogers,
which I've hung on the wall by the calendar Elizabeth brought home from
        Ho Wah Garden.
The calendar was free, though it's filled with interesting photos of Hong
        Kong—the harbor full of ships, glittering banks,
Brazilian-looking clusters of high rises against the lacerated earth and
        jungled hills—not to mention its obvious practicality.

And Kenny?

I guess his picture costs, but can't see why precisely, though it did come with
        a complimentary sheet of recipes,
handy holiday home-cooking tips featuring a wide variety of pineapple
        products, sponsored by Dole, America's favorite,
delicacies such as Pineapple Pizza and Aloha Joes, better known as sloppy
        joes with zesty pineapple for extra zing.

Of course that's Dole pineapple.
America's favorite.
Dole.

Coincidentally,
the first part of my Elvis screen-trilogy
is set in Hong Kong.

A madcap comedy about organized crime.
And the name I picked at random for the Chinese mobsters is Ong.

Only last week I read in the *Times*
that the "Godfather of Chinatown"
is named Bennie Ong.

They're all named Ong,
the most dangerous family in America!

Talk about serendipity.
Thank you Hollywood

for ignoring my very existence!

## II

## THE TRIUMPH OF RATIONALISM

*The Ariadne thread of botany is classification, without which there is chaos.*
*—Linnaeus*

Just beyond the window, the great elm where the squirrels live is shaking
    like kelp in the wind.
Swivelling my chair I can mark its rhythmic parabolas, long slow curves
    like the giant pendulum used to trace
across the floor of the Museum of American History when I was a kid,
    distant in memory as the underside of water,
while this is so close I can feel in my bones the heft of its weight as it
    thumps against the eaves at the apex of each arc.

Oblivious to their mortal danger, the squirrels peer forth at the falling snow
    with the liquid gaze of grandparents
bemused by some obscurely touching act of kindness, which is why I
    worried when the city tree cutters came last summer
but mercifully left this hollow-hearted limb, this cleft nook where they nest
    among leaves and twigs and scraps of paper,

perfectly sheltered, warm and snug,

hell, that nest is probably
warmer than our apartment, yes,
I'm sure it is,

the landlord's too cheap to plug our draughts, wind comes right through
    these rotten sills and casements,
here I sit shivering in three pairs of socks while the squirrels toboggan the
    sidewalk like some comically misplaced species of marsupial,

the snowshoe wallaby
or Great Lakes kangaroo,

though somehow more sinister—note the claws, the fanged grin and
    chiselled jaw, the pooled, clairvoyant eyes.
Only now do I recognize the uncanny resemblance to Murnau's infamous
    expressionistic vampire,

albeit four-legged and somewhat furrier,
yes, it's true,
they are a race of pint-sized

Nosferatu!

&#9670;


This weather reminds me of college, the sort of day I used to skip *Elements
    of Sociology* or *Wittgenstein and the Vienna Circle*
to wander down the Midway in my tattered overcoat and politically correct
    proletarian work boots
past the statues of saintly, latinized Linnaeus and the Unknown Slavic
    Cavalry Hero crowned in crusted snow
to the immense bronze doors of the Museum of Science & Industry by the
    shores of the hard-frozen lake.

How quickly I'd lose myself among those working models of tractors and
    turbines, drill presses and planing lathes,
a history of man's handiwork from flint and adze through hammer and
    chisel to steam locomotive and deep space probe.

What I loved most was the depth and rationality of the catalogue, a
    taxonomic amplitude rivalled only by the menu at Ho Wah Garden,
a lucid precision which seemed to imply that the world could indeed be
    labelled and categorized
into one vast concordance of subject and nomenclature if only there were
    enough display cases to go around.

I think it was this promise that drew the daily flood of field trips and farm
    families from across the Midwest,
a glimpse at the inner workings of their world, the cogs that run the great
    machine, nuts and bolts of the system revealed,
a vision of such faith in the adequacy of the visible, in the efficacy of the
    material, mechanistic world
that my callous skin of intellectual self-certainty was riven right down to
    the molten, cynical core.


&#9670;


There are systems and there are systems.
There are systems within systems.

◆

There is no system!

◆

Chicago itself is a museum of science and industry, a grey mausoleum of
    brawn.

◆

*The world is all that is the case.*

The 20th Century has come down to this.

Everything yields to the woodsman's axe
but still we are not satisfied.
Now we yearn for the vanished trees!

We hunger for that primitive communion,

gathering wild roses by the riverside, dancers in the honey-bloom of irises
    and rye, lotus-eaters among the daffodils,
until, wrung by fierce nostalgic pangs, we cast the blade of reason aside and
    flee into the woods.

That is, we wish we dared relinquish it, wish we even knew the forest for
    the ghosts of illustrious hardwoods that haunt us.

Thus we arrange the wooden blocks
around the scene of the accident
and say *this is the car,*
*this the pedestrian struck down in the crosswalk,*

which however flawlessly logical leaves the bereaved to drink pink
    lemonade and sink alone beneath the millstone of grief.

We are all of us alone,
together,
in our suffering.

At this juncture certain incurable romantics and distinguished French
    semioticians feel themselves compelled to leap into the breech
and are in turn struck down by that reckless jalopy careening backward up
    a one-way street.

I guess they didn't see the sign
in all this snow,
or were unable to apprehend its Saussurean essence,
or simply missed the drift.

Think how much eludes us, in the end, wilful elisions and bad translations,
    collateral damage to indigenous personnel.

Take the "galaxy of black-fry ink-fish," which means squid in bean sauce at
    Ho Wah Garden.
Take the tribesmen of Vanuatu watching from the slopes of their sacred
    volcano for a great white ship laden with cargo—
shoes, shovels, Jeeps, spam—an end to earthly need in the wild beneficence
    of the spirit world.
Take those unlucky backwoods Brazilians who discovered the spherical
    heart of some high-tech hospital CAT-scan machine
and took it home, and prayed to it, and cracked it like a coconut, and ate the
    deadly, radioactive strontium within

because it glowed blue and numinous
with the light of the *orixas*.

Talk about reification!

&#9670;

Take the mytho-practical resistance of the Maori hero, Hono Heke, for
instance. In 1845 Hono Heke deployed his warriors to assault—and un-
intentionally overwhelm—the largest colonial settlement in New
Zealand, *as a diversionary tactic:* that is, in order to accomplish the exploit
Heke always considered more decisive, and on four different occasions
performed, which was to cut down a certain flagpole the British had
erected above the town. "Let us fight," he said, "for the flagpole alone."
                              —Marshall Sahlins, *Islands of History*

◆

Snow.
Plenty of snow.
Regular blizzard out there.
Heap o' snow.


◆


*Apropos the Falling Snow*

   Man in a fur hat
white with Chicago snow—so
   Dostoevskian!


◆


It's so damn snowy I keep expecting Bob Hope
to arrive at the door
with jingling sleigh bells and Dorothy Lamour
and Der Bingle safely in tow,
like a singin' and dancin' Doctor Zhivago
on the *Road to Old New England,* or Muscovy,
or plain old Chicago,
it hardly matters since they're filming on a back lot in Century City,
as this patently bogus blizzard reveals. Brandy
nipped from a silver hip flask,
a counterfeit count at the czar's court unmasked,
a joke and a cuddle to a familiar tune,
tap dance and lindy hop,
jig and a polka
in the back of the troika,
a little soft shoe by the light of the moon.

Whatever happened to those exotic destinations, Bali and Zanzibar and
    Mandalay, an itinerary that reads like the voyage of the *Beagle*
or an Amsterdam spice merchant bound for the Moluccas, the road to
    romance, which is also the path of empire?

What's become of Bob,

our whirling Vishnu hoofing and hamming and yucking it up for the buzz-
    cut boys of sixty years of war,

a man whose life so nearly matches the course of the century, our century, as
     surely as the 17th belonged to the Dutch?

What's become of us,
America,
our Bob-ness, our Self-Hope?

Do all roads lead to the materialistic apotheosis, that miraculous oasis amid
     the golf-bedazzled desert of Palm Springs?


          ◆


Is this the world we danced into creation,
brilliant pebbles,
a thousand points of light?


          ◆


Driven down in anger the snow becomes a shroud or wind-luffed veil torn
     at and buffetted in contradictory billows.
In a lull it disintegrates to particles in suspension, algae or krill, a curtain of
     sediment stirred up by water through a wheel race
or gold miners panning river shallows or the changing tide as it plunges
     through a pass in the outer reef of a ringed atoll.
The trunks of the big trees sway together, bending and rising through the
     swirling blizzard like underwater plants.
The snow-covered branches are intricate as fan-coral, their brilliant mesh as
     lovely as the Astrolabe Reef of Fiji,
as the even greater web of shoals where Captain Cook ran aground in the
     *Endeavour,* June 16, 1770,
all hands saved from sinking by the lucky knob of coral that broke away to
     plug the clear-cut hole in her keel.

Thus is the Great Barrier Reef
discovered by the west.

Seven weeks of repairs on a shore of desolate mangrove and the distant
     smoke of aboriginal fires.
While Cook collected fresh greens against scurvy—palm cabbage and wild
     plantain, purslane and beans and taro—
the men fished for stingrays, shot bandicoots and ducks and dingoes, dug
     giant clams and harpooned turtles in the mud flats.

In the service of scientific inquiry, Joseph Banks hunted down specimens,
     sketched strange birds and unidentified shellfish,
glimpsed, in the thorny underbrush, a mysterious animal—"large as a stag,
     mouse-colored, faster than a greyhound"—
that was, after elaborate effort, shot and killed and taken aboard to be
     skinned, preserved and duly catalogued.

Thus does the kangaroo enter
the ledgers of Natural Science.

◆

The woods and vegetation are as green as in April in Andalucía, and the
song of the little birds might make a man wish never to leave here. The
flocks of parrots that darken the sun and the large and small birds of so
many species are so different from our own that it is a wonder. In addi-
tion, there are trees of a thousand kinds, all with fruit according to their
kind, and they all give off a marvelous fragrance. I am the saddest man
in the world for not knowing what kind of things these are because I am
very sure that they are valuable. I am bringing a sample of everything I
can.

—Columbus' *Log,* October 21, 1492

◆

Few young birds in England have been injured by man, yet all are afraid
of him; many individuals, on the other hand, both at the Galapagos and
at the Falklands, have been injured, but yet have not learned that salu-
tary dread. We may infer from these facts, what havoc the introduction
of any new beast of prey must cause in a country, before the instincts of
the aborigines become adapted to the stranger's craft or power.

—Darwin, *Voyage of the Beagle*

◆

Imagine the great Age of Discovery, enumerating lost continents, glossing
     the empty quadrants of the globe,
renaming tropical islands and equatorial volcanoes for European monarchs
     and snow-bound marchlands,
wonders and marvels of the cosmological bestiary enmeshed in the great net
     of scientific discourse.

Imagine the magnificent moa, kiwi and cassowary, auk and dodo, the
    vanished elephant birds of Madagascar,
the strange case of the kea, as featured last week on the Discovery Channel,
    a species of parrot devolved into a burrow-dwelling pseudorabbit,
driven to the edge of extinction by imported predators—cat, dog, stoat,
    weasel—whose very absence inspired its abandonment of flight.

Imagine an ocean without islands, a planet without the evolutionary quirks
    and behemoths born of isolation's loaded dice.
Imagine the great sea voyages of the Polynesians, 3,000 miles in open boats
    across the undifferentiated Pacific,
though it's true they knew how to read the tides and stars and sea drift,
    cloud-plumes and mist-pennants spun from distant peaks,

the wave patterns islands weave
on the open ocean's loom.

When they settled Easter Island they quarried the mysterious army of *moai*
    and tabular *ahu,* and when they came to New Zealand
they hunted the colossal moa to extinction, and when Captain Cook came
    back once too often they killed him too,

so perhaps it's no surprise that I read in *People* magazine that Sylvester
    Stallone did not even touch ground
while selecting choice building lots on the still-virgin shores of Lanai or
    Kauai or whichever paradisical isle,
merely motioning with his arm from the helicopter as he passed, omen and
    epigone of the once and future onslaught,
as Cook himself was harbinger for the British mercantile colonialism which
    served as host and hatchling for the current *weltwirtschaft* kudzu,
his death, therefore, a kind of consumerist revenge-fantasy, especially as it
    was in all likelihood a British dagger that killed him,
having been loaded and shipped as trade goods for "ye Natives" in 1776, the
    year of American independence,

not to mention the publication
of *The Wealth of Nations.*

♦

What good are daggers against the Invisible Hand?

# III

## Commodity Fetishism in the White City

*Our architecture reflects us, as truly as a mirror.*
> —Louis Sullivan

Looking west from the kitchen the weather is transformed. Storm light
    unrolls like a magic carpet, softens the lowering clouds,
the snow, less ominous, windless, dropping straight down on the alley,
    garages and rooftops geometrically outlined,
smokestacks, water towers, cottonwoods and maples, uniform back porches
    hammered from two-by-fours and unfinished lumber,
the backyard a pillowed expanse extruding elbows and rockers of the
    overturned aluminum patio chairs,
a charnel yard emerging from monsoon mud or a battlefield reclaimed by
    creeping sand dunes.

Thirteen days without sun, terminal overcast stalled above the city like a
    shield to protect us from what we most desire.

Iron grey.
Relentless.
Chicago.

My father tells me there is a depressive syndrome called Seasonal Affective
    Disorder—S.A.D.—which means the midwinter blues,
which means we are, like flowers, heliotropic, subject to solstice, attuned to
    equinox and perihelion,

which means we're even weirder
than we think we are.

Cushion of snow on the window ledge, whistling tea kettle, steam like the
    ghost of Hot Chocolate Past:
feels like a day off from school, license to curl up in blankets and watch
    "The Price Is Right" until Mom comes home.

    ♦

Hey, I think I'll enjoy this
tasty repast
in front of the tube!

Let's see now: leftover
Chinese
or liverwurst and swiss?

♦

Look, that dogfood's packed
with real beef gravy!

Will the celebrity spokesperson eat it?

I'm still waiting for the advertising boys to break this taboo, leap this low
    hurdle, cross the Rubicon of bestiality
and compel Robert Urich or Lorne Green or whichever down-on-his-luck
    former primetime star
to plunge a silver fork into those luscious nuggets and savor the rich, hearty
    flavor of all-beef goodness

just like Fido!

After all, if I won't eat it, why should he?
If it's good enough for my dog, it's good enough for me.

Such a small, such a beautifully small,
such an infinitesimally
gorgeous

abyss.

♦

Of course, meat was Chicago's first great industry,

a virtual monopoly controlled by the South Side packinghouses, Gustavus
    Swift and Phillip Armour and the rest of their cutthroat cartel,
their visionary manipulation of consumer psychology, the pickling vats and
    offal heaps laid bare by Upton Sinclair,
vast fleets of refrigerator cars at the Union Stockyards manned by rock-
    bottom immigrant labor,

the strong-shouldered muscle the city was built upon,
the capital accumulation by which it was built,

a real killing,
anyway you slice it.

If New York is an apple,
Chicago is pure sausage.

Chicago is liverwurst.
Chicago is lumber, sowbellies, soybeans, freight trains.
Chicago is the nexus where pigs and cows become puts and calls, where
      corn and copper become shorts and corners,

where wheat transforms into paper promises
premised on possible productivity,
which is to say, *the future,*

all by means of one simple equation.

Cattle drive, feedlot, slaughterhouse: Board of Trade.
Clearcut, logjam, lumberyard: Board of Trade.
Amber waves, gristmill, Wonder Bread: Board of Trade.

It's a form of modern alchemy,
a public sacrament,
an open secret!

It's a quick trip on the El to the ornate observation balconies above the
      primal trading pits in the Loop,
where you can witness the literal transmogrification of the fruits of earthly
      labor into abstract quanta
by gangs of men signifying with frantic gestures the private glyphs of their
      transnumerative calculus,

a scene which never fails to remind me
of apes learning sign language
on the Discovery Channel,

their hierarchy and ritual deference,
slow mastery of sign and indicator,
the pathos of their struggle to articulate desire—

GIVE APPLE KOMBI

Chicago has an apple for Kombi,
if the price is right!

Chicago is ready to talk turkey.

Chicago is a Great Ape House gone bananas,
a Hanseatic citadel in hog heaven,
a mercantile carnation pinned to the lake's lapel,
a magic hat from which the rabbit of capital is pulled,
a portal into the realm of money itself,

and as in all border towns the locals grow rich off the unwary travellers
     they smilingly fleece and service,
and woe unto he who suffers the perils of fortune unincorporated into the
     greater risk pool of the system.

◆

In December 1836, an enterprising local miller bought up more than a
thousand hogs from Sugar Creek farms and drove them down the road
to American Bottom. Twenty miles south of the Creek a sudden drastic
drop in temperature caught him and his men, threatening them with
killing cold. As they raced in panic for the shelter of a nearby cabin, their
hogs began desperately to pile up on each other for warmth. Those on
the inside smothered, those on the outside froze, creating a monumental
pyramid of ham, frozen on the hoof. The marketing experiment was a
dead loss and the miller financially destroyed.
                                        —John Mack Faragher, *Sugar Creek*

◆

So Chicago grew
and grew fat
off the fat of the heartland.

So it is still, more or less unchanged in its bluntly commercial convictions.

Rich men wear fur coats in the streets because the weather is cold and they
     are rich.

Factory workers drive Oldsmobiles because Oldsmobiles are better than
     Buicks and they don't make Packards anymore.
Unemployed factory workers move out of the city because the only place
     hiring is Wal-Mart and it's cheaper out there in the hinterlands of
     exurbia.

Chicago is your basic meat and potatoes.
Chicago is white bread.
Chicago is a monumental pyramid of ham.

♦

When man Vanuatu brought the pig with him from New Guinea thou-
sands of years ago, he probably brought also the concept of it as the most
valuable currency. With pigs he could ascend in status, with pigs he
could acquire wives, with pigs he could pay for the services of sorcerers
and artisans. The pig may not have been the most portable currency
ever devised, but in Western Melanesia it still remains the most highly
prized.

                              —Norman and Ngaire Douglas, *Vanuatu: A Guide*

♦

This train of thought
is spoiling
my lunch. That's the problem

with liverwurst:
twenty minutes later you're
hungry again.

♦

Speaking of ham,
Bob Hope has always been big in Chicago.
Seven shows a day at the Stratford Theater, still glamorous

in 1946. Seven shows!
The man is nothing if not a fanatic,
an indomitable trooper in the old joke factory, a faded rose

of a star-spangled performaholic,
although, like so much that we consider American,
he's an imported model, not a true domestic.

Son of a hard-drinking immigrant stone mason,
Bob passed through Ellis Island early,
en route from Bristol to his new home in Cleveland,

where he evinced a precocious talent for comedy,
a ready facility for cutting a rug,
changed his name from the original Leslie

and thus became Bob Hope the Buckeye street pug,
Bob Hope the shill at the Alhambra pool hall,
Bob Hope the wisecracking street-corner thug.

Quit school at sixteen to work in his uncle's butcher stall,
hard-knuckled, hungry, lean and pale
from the long days of ox blood and entrails,

sour odor of meat beneath his fingernails
during tap-dance lessons at Sojack's Dance Academy
on Lake Erie evenings grey as a lunch pail,

a tenth grade dropout with the gift of gab, an affinity
for hard work, and a dream
to escape blue-collar Ohio, a trinity

familiar to every immigrant's son, the dream
of new world wealth and glory,
the American Dream.

And the rest, as they say, is history.
Which happens to be
our story.

♦

Have you noticed there's nothing on TV anymore?

Liposuction. Public prayer. Cajun food. Korean cartoons. Jane Goodall's
    chimps. The Congress.

History repeats itself.
So, too, the History Channel.

Again Grant's army encamped before Vicksburg.
Again the Gold Rush, again the Gilded Age.
Again the Wobblies, again Black Friday, again the New Deal, again *Enola Gay.*

On CNBC today, word that "gourmet pet food" is America's newest
    multibillion dollar industry.
On CNN, an increase in global malnutrition; 40,000 children die of hunger
    and its attendant diseases every day.

Which is not to say there is any particular correlation between these
    contemporaneous pronouncements,
not to say the good citizens of Chicago would rather their dogs eat Veal and
    Kidney Morsels than the children of Pakistan eat rice,
not to say we can even encompass the human implications of these binary
    blips aswim in the inundation of the great data flow,
the Sea of Information from which they have arisen like walruses heaved
    up on some high blue shelf of the Malthusian iceberg.

     ♦

I thought squirrels were supposed to hibernate.
Isn't that what they say on the Discovery Channel?
Isn't that what "the industrious hoarding of acorns" is all about?

So what's with this rigmarole in the branches?

Here's one clambering up through six inches of snow, struggling to drag a
    frozen newspaper back to its nest,
a bedraggled sheath of ads for cars or maybe tires, steel-belted radials from
    Sears or Montgomery Ward.

Alas, poor Sears, the state's largest employer, the world's tallest building and
    the city's most obvious landmark,
an unrentable white elephant boxing the Loop in sovereign shadow. Once
    upon a time they ruled the world!

Once upon a time Chicago was the general store for half the nation, not just
    day-trippers in from Wisconsin and Indiana but all those within reach
    of the mighty catalogues,

all those bicycles and reapers and mason jars shipped out to pickle the beets
    and preserve the plums of Oklahoma, Kansas, Minnesota and the
    Dakotas.

◆

By the dawn of the new century, the Montgomery Ward catalog con-
tained 1200 pages and 17000 illustrations, offering no fewer than 70000
separate items for sale. . . . The firms' yearly postal money order busi-
ness was greater than that of entire cities like Cincinnati, New Orleans,
or San Francisco. . . . By 1900, Montgomery Ward and Sears, Roebuck
were the two greatest merchandising organizations in the world.
                          —William Cronon, *Nature's Metropolis*

◆

When I was a kid I'd walk up to Sears to buy just about anything—

ballpoint pens or school notebooks,
a new sled, leaf bags,
a lawn mower or Doobie Brothers album.

Today, I'd as soon shoot myself as shop at Sears!

Today one must navigate daunting loops of expressway misnomers out to
    some suburban circumlocution
in order to ransack the latest jumbo, discount, wholesale Wal- or K- or
    What-the-Hey-Mart,
which is not so much a store as a merchandizing organization disguised as
    an aircraft hangar lumped full of bulk commodities.

◆

Chicago itself is a merchandizing organization
disguised as an aircraft hangar
lumped full of bulk commodities.

◆

Yes, that's true.
It is.
We are.

Materialism is our genius; must we bow down our heads in shame
    therefore?
Why apologize for seeking fulfillment in the satiation of our hungers?
What engine drives human history if not the elevation of physical comfort?
What other principle conforms to the contours of individual desires?
Is it not our Jeffersonian right and obligation to pursue the fleeting figure of
    happiness?

♦

Happiness

I asked professors who teach the meaning of life to tell me what is
    happiness.
And I went to famous executives who boss the work of thousands of
    men.
They all shook their heads and gave me a smile as though I was trying to
    fool with them.
And then one Sunday afternoon I wandered out along the Desplaines
    river
And I saw a crowd of Hungarians under the trees with their women
    and children and a keg of beer and an accordion.
                                                        —Carl Sandburg

♦

Yes, Carl, how beautiful
a poem,
how telling, how fine.

But can we subsist on a diet of accordion music and raw profusion?
Is the solace of the material enough to sustain us?
At what cost has it been purchased?
Don't we crave a more elusive amplitude, a hunger no less intense for being
    nameless?
Is it possible to fix a common focus with such singularity of vision?

When I look out my window, when I look not to look but to see, even the
    most elemental forms and objects are shaded with hermeneutical
    nuance,
the unsaid, the understood, subtexts half-buried by this blizzard of the
    incomprehensible,

a world of circumstance and utter contingency invested with a deep and
    apparent historical sheen.

In these arcane graffiti sprayed across the Baptist church are encoded the
    territorial markings of the local Chicano street gangs,
children of Oaxaca and Michoacán displaced to the frozen verge of Lake
    Michigan,
their scrawled logos imbued with intricacies of signification akin to Mayan
    sunstones or the bird-man petroglyphs of Easter Island.

In these wooden houses and brick three-flats is depicted the evolution and
    degradation of the American city,
our hegemonic apogee and concomitant deliquescence, the wildfire of
    industrialization that fueled Chicago's growth,
the development of the consumer economy and the invention of the
    balloon-frame building method,
a tradition of relentless reduction to cheaper and faster means through the
    turbo-engine of mass production.

In the Housing Authority high-rise perched anomalously on the corner of
    Clark Street is written the victory of New Deal liberalism and the
    failure of its utopian social engineering,
not to mention the aesthetic capitulation to Bauhaus hideosity its yellow-
    brick conformity embodies,
and in so far as half of its inhabitants are retired black city workers, and the
    other half ancient Japanese widows,
it reifies simultaneously the memory of the Nisei internment camps and the
    postwar movement of African-Americans to the manufacturing centers
    of the north,

which in turn encompasses a brief history of organized labor,
and how the blues came up the river from Mississippi,
and the relativity of our Constitutional liberties,
and the dark imponderable of slavery,

and a deeper strata of humanistic yearning in the age-old migration of
    populations in search of material betterment.

Material betterment!

I guess you could say
the writing
is on the wall, *hermano.*

You could say the writing is the wall,

our homes are our castles,
our bodies our temples,

so what metaphor must the city we live in describe?

What girders underlie the construction of the dream?
What marvels of engineering, what existential architecture?
What wrecking ball or hidden rot even now betokens its deconstruction?

If what we build speaks for us, what does Chicago say?

What's written in Louis Sullivan's damascened grillework, the Sears
    behemoth, the public housing battlements, the suburbs' ever increasing
    dominion?
What texts are affixed to the shingle roofs of the endless blocks of Back-of-
    the-Yards bungalows?
What utilitarian tunes would the warped beams of this tired house hum?

What about what we haven't built,
what's been lost,
what we've built and then torn down,

the mile-high skyscraper of Frank Lloyd Wright, the bulldozed stockyards
    and Comiskey Park,
red wagons of waffle vendors at the Water Street Market and Delta
    bluesmen stomping around Maxwell Street trash fires,
the palisade of old Fort Dearborn where the Pottawatomie came to trade
    for blankets, hatchets, whiskey and beads?

What about the White City,

the World's Columbian Exposition master-planned by Daniel Burnham to
    serve as Chicago's debutante cotillion,
a prolix effulgence of fin-de-siècle flotsam announcing the end of the 19th
    Century seen as the Age of Progress through Industry?

If the 7-11 is a minnow, and Wal-Mart a bluefin tuna, the White City was
    Moby Dick.
If the 7-11 is a slot machine, and Wal-Mart a bingo parlor, the White City
    was Las Vegas.

If the 7-11 is a glittering chapel—like the beautiful Santuario at Chimayo—
    and Wal-Mart a sturdy cinder block church of solid suburban
    parishioners,

then the White City was a metropolis of neoclassical cathedrals raised up to
    the Gods of Materialism themselves—

Manufactures, Machinery,
Electricity, Transportation, Agriculture,
Forestry, Fisheries, Mines.

Such were the pavilions wherein was gathered every conceivable artifact
    and innovation of national origin or adoptive ancestry,

every all-American doodad, gizmo, gimcrack and curlicue,
and those of the various individual states,
and those of whichever nation or homeland cared to participate,

all and sundry jam-packed into some dozen
bulging Palladian pleasure domes,
an urban dreamscape of wings, naves, galleries and transepts,
lagoons, ponds, basins, bridges,
wedding-cake fountains and creamsicle statuary,

plus scores of lesser Beaux Arts repositories,
plus the carnival clutter and anthropological detritus of the Midway.

The murals in the Woman's Building were painted by Mary Cassat.
Louis Sullivan designed the Transportation Pavilion, and later denounced it
    as an exercise in sentimental retrospection.
Eugene V. Debs saw the whole assemblage as tribute to the laborers that
    built it, among them Elias Disney, Walt's father, driving nails into the
    prototypical Magic Kingdom.
Henry Adams came back twice to plumb its mysteries; William Dean
    Howells found nirvana reflected within its Golden Door.
Frederick Douglass addressed "The Race Problem in America" on
    "Colored People's Day" when the vendors sold watermelon in naked
    mockery.
Thorstein Veblen invented socioeconomics to explain the daily spectacle out
    the window of his office in the newly-christened University.
Frederick Jackson Turner announced the closing of the American frontier
    in his famous derivation from 1890 census data,

the first to use punch cards for rapid tabulation,
the binary egg from which the computer was hatched,

thereby yoking the past with the future,
that century with this,
the Information Age with the vanishing Era of the Heroic Individual,

whose incorporation into the body politic was symbolically recapitulated in
   this act of appropriation, quantification, and mythopoeic enshrinement.

Which is why cowboys blame bureaucrats and not barbed wire for their
   troubles.
Which is why IBM was once the Tabulating-Recording Machine Company.
Which is why thirty million people visited the White City in the half-year it
   was open.
Which is why we speak of it as a watershed.
Which is an uncomfortable metaphor alongside the Great Lakes.


♦


Since Noah's ark, no such Babel of loose and ill-joined, such vague and
ill-defined and unrelated thoughts and half-thoughts and experimental
outcries as the Exposition, had ever ruffled the surface of the lakes.

Chicago asked in 1893 for the first time the question whether the Amer-
ican people knew where they were driving.

Chicago was the first expression of American thought as a unity; one
must start there.
                                   —Henry Adams, *The Education of Henry Adams*


♦


Anyway, six months later they
demolished it,
or let it go to arson,

every pergola, proscenium, collonade and cornice,

so much unfinished confectionary,
so much frosting on a cake of illusion.

Beneath the facade the White City was built not of brick or granite but of
    sculpted plaster over lath and beams,
a temporary contrivance unfit to weather the winter, meant to look
    beautiful but not to last,
as if they'd constructed Disney World from Lego blocks and Lincoln logs
    and torn it all down at the first sign of rain,

as if it were merely a form of mass hallucination,
a collective vision of a heaven so imminent
its electric glow lit the contours of the century's horizon
with the glitter of a thousand elysian fields,

as it still does, in reverse, for us, looking backward,

a quixotic flame like a firefly encased in viscous amber,
a token of everything we have become in a dialect we no longer speak,
a beacon as perfect and irretrievable as a dream.

♦

Newly arrived and totally ignorant of the Levantine languages, Marco
Polo could express himself only with gestures, leaps, cries of wonder
and of horror, animal barkings or hootings, or with objects he took from
his knapsacks—ostrich plumes, pea-shooters, quartzes—which he
arranged in front of him like chessmen. Returning from the missions on
which Kublai sent him, the ingenious foreigner improvised pan-
tomimes that the sovereign had to interpret: one city was depicted by the
leap of a fish escaping the cormorant's beak to fall into a net; another city
by a naked man running through fire unscorched; a third by a skull, its
teeth green with mold, clenching a round, white pearl. The Great Khan
deciphered the signs, but the connection between them and the places
visited remained uncertain; he never knew whether Marco wished to
enact an adventure that had befallen him on his journey, an exploit of
the city's founder, the prophecy of an astrologer, a rebus or a charade to
indicate a name. But, obscure or obvious as it might be, everything
Marco displayed had the power of emblems, which, once seen, cannot
be forgotten or confused. In the Khan's mind the empire was reflected
in a desert of labile and interchangeable data, like grains of sand, from
which there appeared, for each city and province, the figures evoked by
the Venetian's logogriphs.

                             —Italo Calvino, *Invisible Cities*

City of concrete, city of illusion, how to decipher such dialectical
    ambiguity?
How can I reconcile my affection with my anger, my need to criticize with
    my desire to praise?
If there's only one Chicago, which is it: Thorstein Veblen's or Milton
    Freidman's, Gene Debs' or Mayor Daley's,
the White City, the Grey City, the black city abandoned to sift through the
    ashes?

If no man is an island, why was Daniel Burnham buried on one?
If even this utopian visionary elects for himself eternal isolation what hope
    can there be for any commonweal?
What does it mean that Louis Sullivan ended in impoverished oblivion,
    tormented by the shadows of the skyscrapers he invented?
Can it be a mere coincidence that the balloon-frame building method was
    developed by a man named Snow—

or else Augustine Deodat Taylor,
depending on which source you credit?

Have I mentioned that the Museum of Science & Industry is in fact the last
    vestige of the Columbian Exposition,
the former Palace of Fine Arts at the great fair, the only one of the White
    City's temples built of actual stone?
Or that Lincoln logs were invented by John Lloyd Wright, first son of
    famous Frank?
What sort of diminutive Oedipal revenge is this: Laius stabbed to death by a
    toothpick, modernism brought down by Lilliputian arrows?

How can I account for my love of this place?
Is it simply nostalgia, that I was born here, that my son, so soon, presumably
    will be?
Could it really be as simple as fathers and sons, that ancient, atavistic, blood-
    weary principle?

What voice is this that issues from the deep well of the past?
Who calls to me from that vast assemblage?
All this, all this—

and what?

## IV

## THE ROAD TO UTOPIA

*California is a garden of Eden,*
  *A paradise to live in or see*
    *But believe it or not*
  *You won't find it so hot*
  *If you ain't got the do-re-me.*

—*Woody Guthrie*

What is it people see in Bob Hope? Or saw? Or found reflected? Or hoped
    to find?
Why did they line up for all those happily ham-fisted movies, the USO
    shows, the vaudeville act, the cornball radio and TV routines?
Why do three kitchen spatulas hang suspended like lonely aluminum leaves
    from the neighbor's barren crabapple tree?
How do they get the Szechuan string beans to stay so crunchy at Ho Wah
    Garden?
Why do you never see a dead pigeon in the city, well maybe a few, but not
    in any proportion to their numbers?
Where are the babies, where are the toddlers and the teenage pigeons?
Why are there no dead squirrels in Chicago?

Ah, but here again I equivocate.

I did see a squirrel drop once,
from a precarious limb,
never to rise again on this green earth.

And one squashed flat by a delivery van.
(I think it was the UPS man.)

And then there was the one whose heart gave out in the squirrel trap I set
    on my landlord's instructions,

lips drawn back, stiff as the grave,
bristling with lost vitality.

Which the landlord claims is not supposed to happen.

According to him it's no problem to catch and then release them, they're
    such a nuisance, tearing up his attic, not to mention the health hazard,

and anyway they're better off at the "forest preserve," which is somewhere
     in the suburbs, he's a little vague, but not to worry,
all of which sounds great until I check the peanut butter bait to find the
     very first one has given up the ghost,

frozen in terror,
tiny heart shocked to a halt.

Which it turns out is not so unlikely after all.

Yeah, that happens a lot,
the landlord says, matter of factly,

but urges me to continue with the "removal program,"

repeating his fantastically unlikely depiction of their suburban refuge with
     fawning concern as if it was a veritable paradise out there,
a pastoral wonderland of ageless shade trees and precollected acorns, as if he
     was the Leo Buscaglia of the rodent world.

Not that I am deaf
to the logic
of his grievance.

Those lovable tree-vampires have gouged a hole right through the fake-
     shingle siding, just beneath the gutter,
through which I hear them scratch their way into the attic to filch pink
     Corning fiberglass insulation by the mouthful,
lugging it from roof to branch to limb, where it catches in little bud-sized
     clumps that bloom, after rainfall, as hairy red flowers in the branches,

like something from the Amazon,

a newly-discovered carnivorous tea rose, a rare species of canopy orchid
     rescued by botanists from rising flood waters.

Or snowdrifts.

◆

"It was not I who killed you," the Finnish bear hunter used to say, "and
     not any of my brothers either. You yourself stumbled in the forest, you

yourself slipped from the branch, that is how your golden body burst
and your stomach full of berries."

—Hans Peter Duerr, Dreamtime

◆

Must be something afoot with the Postal Service in the neighborhood, a
    new superintendent or get-tough policy.
Look at this flatbed truck driving gingerly down the block, packed full of
    shiny new government-blue mailboxes.
Just last week two men came with rivet-guns and planted one on the corner
    of Halsted Street.

I assume it will grow up
to be a post office.

Look at our poor mailman, suffering the pangs of hypothermia or frostbite
    as he staggers up the street like Chaplin in The Gold Rush,
like Jack London lugging his earthly possessions to the Yukon or some '49er
    crossing the Sierras
or those picturesque Brazilians bearing ore-sacks and wicker baskets into
    the open pit at Serra Pelada,

Dantean spectres from the deep mud of the dream.

Imagine what stamped benediction, what metered mark of grace he might
    be bringing me today:

good word from Hollywood about my screenplay;
a Guggenheim; a genius grant;
an NEA!

Any piece of parcel post could bear my silver slipper, my invitation to the
    ball and a dance with Ed McMahon.
I can see me now, sharing a laugh with Letterman, hoking and joking with
    Arsenio or Conan, holding forth from the center square.

◆

Isn't that my picture
on the cover
of People magazine!

◆

But wait.
Hold on a minute.
What would I do if it all came true?

I'd have to say
yes, no?
Or else no, yes?

Am I a stooge of the popular culture machine?

I want it
all! I want
it all. I
want it all?

◆

I am a veritable
Walt Whitman
of ambivalence.

◆

But then, ambivalence
is a luxury
affordable to few, while

utopianism
is an
American tradition!

The cadences of the past unroll like names of toys, a child's puzzle-pieces in
      the rain, overtures of wind in the stately trees

above the City on the Hill,
above the Great Awakening,
above a nation or mighty congregation

of tried and true believers—

faith healers and snake handlers, circuit riders and holy rollers, Shakers and
    Rappites and Perfectionists,
Jonathan Edwards and Roger Williams, William Miller and Joseph Smith,
    Mary Baker Eddy and Johann Beissel, the Faustus of Conestoga,
who preached in tongues and reversed his argument if any nodded assent,
    "to demonstrate the incomprehensibility of God's truth,"

which even at the best of times is mystifying,
muffled with portent or possibly ear wax,
or have we simply grown harder of hearing?

There goes the CD.
Time to face the music.

In the digital silence comes the whispered call of a dove, followed by the
    raucous reply of a crow hidden in some attic of the storm.

Coo. Caw.
Hush of the snow fall.
Invisible voices, invisible wings.

        ◆

I hope Elizabeth gets home OK in all this snow.
Look at the car.
Buried.

        ◆


*After Buson*

    Parked cars—
snow
    in place of hubcaps!

        ◆


An explorer in Greenland once terrified himself by seeking refuge from
a storm in the lee of what he first took to be mounds of snow-covered
earth. They were muskoxen, and they began to stand up as he walked
over them.

                                —Barry Lopez, *Arctic Dreams*


                                                                    47

◆

But then, perception is everything.

Think of Cortés in Mexico.
Think of Cook in Hawaii.
Think of Dan Quayle in Samoa,

dismissing the grievances of the proud hereditary chieftains with a haughty
     wave of his Hoosier hand:

"You look like happy campers to me."

Think of the conquistadors' insane exploits in pursuit of El Dorado or
     Cíbola or the island of Queen Calafia,
whatever legendary City of Gold they saw reflected in the mists or heat-
     waves beyond the next blue valley or ridgeline.
Think of Joseph Smith divining the location of buried treasure in the
     Indian mounds around Palmyra, New York,
before confronting in person the angel Moroni, who begat his
     transformation into divine prophet and martyr of the Latter-day Saints.
Think of *The Road to Utopia,* in which Hope and Crosby play a pair of
     stranded vaudevillians mistaken for desperadoes

in the midst of the Klondike gold rush!

Think of "The Miracle Tree of Little Havana."

◆

A 92-year-old man said sap from the just-trimmed tree cured his
cataracts on Good Friday. After the "weeping tree" made the radio air-
waves, the faithful flooded the neighborhood. By Easter weekend, the
tree had been chainsawed to a stump by entrepreneurs who sold it in
pieces.
                                                  —The Miami *Herald,* September 20, 1994

◆

What is it with these two,

faith and profit,
God and lucre,
dove and crow,

material fortune and spiritual salvation paradoxically conjoined like
    Siamese twins we are forever confusing the names of—

is it Bob and Bing
or Bing and Bob?—

no coin without an inverse.

This morning, walking Elizabeth to the El on Belmont in a light,
    premonitory dusting of snow,
a man stepping suddenly from the shadows beneath the trestles said "This is
    for you—for *you*," just so, emphatically,
and thrust a pamphlet into my gloved hands, by which it was crumpled into
    a pocket while I kissed Elizabeth good-bye,
dashed into the station to buy a *Tribune* from the Pakistani newsstand
    operator and back out against the flood tide of commuters,
and so happily homeward, reading about Michael Jordan, kick the snow
    from my boots at the door, up the stairs to our apartment,
off boots, in the door, down the hall, off hat and gloves, into the kitchen,
    coat on rack, scarf into coat pocket,
which must be when it tumbled forth to the floor, from whence I now
    recover and face again its insinuating portent of doom.

◆

*What if you died today?*

Even while reading this tract, you could be having a slight pain in your
chest or head; but
WITHIN A FEW HOURS YOU WILL BE DEAD!
You might be in good health, but
ON THE WAY HOME YOU WILL BE KILLED.
THESE WILL BE THE LAST WORDS YOU EVER READ!

*YOU CAN'T ESCAPE DEATH*

No matter how good you are, God says, YOU DESERVE TO BURN
IN THE LAKE OF FIRE FOREVER & EVER!

Jesus, put your trust in the Almighty
Saviour, I say do ye yield unto me, do ye . . .

(something from Ephesians, obliterated by melting snow in the creases)

IT IS NOT COINCIDENCE THAT YOU ARE READING THIS TRACT
*God planned it just for you,*
this could be

YOUR LAST WARNING

♦

Now I ask you, is that terrifying?
What manner of gospel is this?
Unreconstructed hellfire and brimstone?

Certainly not what I'm used to receiving
from the kindly dispensers of the Watchtower,
or the Moonies, or nicely-dressed Mormons on bicycles.

Not even the standard apocalyptic ire mailman Rick is wont to deliver—
righteous gyrations from Young Republicans
or rumblings of eco-catastrophe from Greenpeace—

though today, for all his herculean effort,
the mail brings nothing but lingerie catalogues,
"sup-r-valu" pizza deals, and a very special

URGENT MESSAGE—

YOU HAVE WON!
YOU ARE ALREADY A LUCKY WINNER!
DON'T MAKE US GIVE YOUR MONEY TO SOMEONE ELSE!

—informing me that I WILL RECEIVE a prize worth up to ONE MILLION
 DOLLARS CASH,
or maybe a brand new JAGUAR, or else a LUXURY CRUISE, or a VCR, or a
 Taiwanese watch, or possibly a tote bag,
if my entry blank matches the previously selected Grand Prize Winners
 code,

the odds of which are fully disclosed per government regulation
    as precisely twenty million to one.

Oh well.
Easy come, easy go.
Ed McMahon giveth and Ed McMahon taketh away.

I've never fully understood the allure of gambling anyway, never lasted
    beyond a handful of nickels in the lobby of the Tropicana.

Why do people do it?
Don't they understand the inflexible odds stacked against them?
Does the weight of probability mean nothing?
Would you plant your money in a hole in the ground if I told you a silver-
    dollar tree would grow there?
Would you send it to a man on TV if he promised to tame the lions of your
    sorrow?
Would you build a runway in the jungle to lure the phantom cargo of the
    spirit world?
Would you construct a great cathedral to gain the favor of the Lord?
Would you pan for holy gold in the rivers of the spirit?


                    ♦


The gold-digger in the ravines of the mountains is as much a gambler as
his fellow in the saloons of San Francisco. What difference does it make
whether you shake dirt or shake dice? If you win, society is the loser.
                            —Thoreau, "Life Without Principle"


                    ♦


At least gold mining is an activity, an enterprise, something to do, though
    the odds are typically far-fetched,
the few legitimate lucky strikes outweighed by the legions of failures, the
    vast, silent, empty-handed majority,
those broken and embittered '49ers too poor or distraught to return home
    losers in the "Great California Lottery,"
straggling back down to the bay from their overnight boomtowns and
    scurvy-ridden mining camps,

Iowa Hill, Georgia Slide, Dixie Valley, Michigan Bluffs,
Dutch Flat, Irish Creek, Chinese Camp, Kanaka Bar,

not to mention Stringtown,
Placerville,
Volcano and You Bet.

◆

Oh, Matilda, oft is the night when laying alone on the hard ground with
a blanket under me and one over me that my thoughts go back to Ohio
and I think of you and wish myself with you. But I am willing to stand it
all to make enough to get us a home and so I can be independent of some
of the darned sonsabitches that felt themselves above me because I was
poor. Cuss them.

—David Dewolf, July 30, 1850
(from J.S. Holliday, *And the World Rushed In*)

◆

Thus was conceived,
by accident,
our only legitimate City of Gold:

San Francisco.

Because the real mother lode was never in the braided flats and gravel bars
    of those impetuous Sierra rivers,

but in the bellies and backs of the miners themselves.

In the goldfields a boiled egg cost 75¢;
two acres of onions sold for $2,000;
one woman claimed to have made $18,000

selling apple pies to the miners!

And the gold mine of commerce was an irony not lost upon the Mormons,
    driven to Utah by whatever oxymoronic glue
had bound them together throughout their persecution and earlier
    migration across the Midwest to Nauvoo—

a lovely town on a bluff above the river,
about three hours south,
Elizabeth and I have driven it;

there's a reconstructed frontier village
among a grove of majestic cottonwoods
in the Mississippi flood plain—

so that, when the gold rush unleashed its secular pilgrimage, those wagon
    trains bound for glory at Sutter's Mill
found the emigrant trails already serviced by Mormon farmers selling hay
    reaped in high mountain meadows,
and ferry service across the wild western rivers from entrepreneurs sent
    forth by Brigham Young to charge whatever the market would bear!

Thus was born Salt Lake City,
Pillar of Faith
in the heart of Deseret.

Thus was born the Golden State.
Thus was born the truckstop.

        ◆

> Raisins may be the best part of a cake; but a bag of raisins is not better
> than a cake; and someone who is in a position to give us a bag full of
> raisins still can't bake a cake with them, let alone do something better.
>            —Wittgenstein, *Culture and Value*

        ◆

> I've enjoyed doing those television commercials, for example with Tex-
> aco. They take time, however, and on those days there's no golf for me.
> When I'm taping commercials, it's impossible for me to do anything
> else. It's not like a personal appearance. Then I can play golf, because I
> know my act and I can ad-lib some stuff. But in taping I have to pay at-
> tention. There are so many details.
>     —Bob Hope, *Confessions of a Hooker: My Lifelong Love Affair with Golf*

        ◆

James Marshall, the man who began the California gold rush, lost his state
    pension due to public drunkenness and died in obscurity,
hard by the sight of his accidental discovery, in Coloma, Eldorado County,
    along the banks of the American River.

John A. Sutter died penniless in a Washington hotel room, petitioning the
    government for restitution of lands and property stolen by squatters.
The day Marshall cried eureka, the San Francisco peninsula was home to a
    few hundred farmers and itinerant fishermen;

two years later, a city of 30,000 and rising.

After a year of snowbound, Social Darwinistic struggle, Jack London
    abandoned his dream of Yukon wealth,
but gained even greater fortune and fame off the tales of his adventures,
    though never contentment,
in search of which he set off in the *Snark* for the South Pacific but found
    instead malarial torpor,
returning home in ruined health to watch his life burn down in a haze of
    smoke and morphine-flame at his majestic estate above Sonoma.

Fourth in the series of seven road films, *The Road to Utopia* is the one where
    Bob finally gets the girl—Dottie Lamour, of course—
after ninety minutes of misadventures with back-stabbing beaver trappers
    and Bud the lovable Saint Bernard,
while Bing is lost on a treacherous ice floe, but turns up years later in an
    ironic denouement having at last struck it rich in Alaska.

◆

Anecdotes then are among the principal products of a culture's repre-
sentational technology, mediators between the undifferentiated succes-
sion of local moments and a larger strategy toward which they can only
gesture.

—Stephen Greenblatt, *Marvellous Possessions*

◆

Modern poetry, however, is filled with what we should otherwise call
"pointless anecdotes," or anecdotes of which the only point could be,
"This is a kind of thing that happens."

—Barbara Herrnstein Smith, *Poetic Closure*

◆

And the szechuan string beans at Ho Wah Garden?
    They keep that recipe a family secret.

54

And "The Weeping Tree of Little Havana"?
    You get what you pay for, as they say.
And the spatulas in the empty branches?
    Patience: they may yet ripen into silver dollars.


                ◆


Why are there no dead squirrels in Chicago?

It's a trick question!
There are.
You just don't read about them

in *People* magazine.

# V

## CARGO CULTS IN THE REPUBLIC OF DREAMS

*The United States themselves are essentially the greatest poem.*
*—Whitman*

In the sheer, exacting mirror of the glass; in the rills and daisy chains of
    lucent frost that web the inner surface of the window;
in each flake as it flattens momentarily to view before gusting away,
    gravitating earthward or drawn back into the whirling anonymity of
    the storm;
within each individual crystal, each facet, each pane, I see the world
    imperfectly reflected, and I see myself,
flawed and shadowed, captive within each image, and superimposed across
    the vision of the whole.

Slow as hovercraft, yellow taxis glide down the block, churning the snow to
    tire-treads of sludge.
The sidewalk, trodden by hardy dog walkers, shovelled by overzealous
    attendants of public safety, seems passable,

even in this storm
the path to the lake is easily found,

what's difficult is to cipher the images held within its matrix: brash ice and
    frazil ice, rime ice and pancake ice;
glare ice that rides the water's body like a fat man's belly in skintight
    clothes; ice lobes, ice pipes, ice lenses;
crags and pillars and sculpted fragments; hieroglyphs for which we possess
    no index or Rosetta stone;
a tidal dialogue of comings and goings; a phenomenological syntax of
    swaths and flows.

And even when the first true thaw arrives, no simple matter in this season
    of iron resolve, even after months of restless wind,
pollen storms and cloacal fog, false leads and sweet murmuring, a dream, a
    knock at the door, any sudden movement in the night,

when spring comes to Chicago
in all its flush and dilatory glory,

even then, come May, come June, when the water returns to mere mute
    imperfect calm,
when we walk the wave-bitten granite and see the city's skeleton revealed as
    by X ray against prairie sky,
count stones in the shallows round as goose eggs, smooth as loons or peals of
    laughter, cuneiform duck prints along the marshy verge,
harbors of sailboats, tiger lilies and water hyacinth, tide marks and growth
    rings, loose billows of April rain

or the ripples of clouds reflected in summer water,

even when we glimpse, for a moment, this sense of pattern, of some deeper
    structure, a framework, warp and woof,
who can say, even then, whether what we perceive is the actual weaving or
    a skein of random, colorfast threads?

What I see more nearly resembles the amorphous diversity of the snowfall,
    a shifting association of individual particles,

grouped or scattered, linear or cyclonic,

now fierce, now calm,
now purposeful, now lost.

If such is our society, who are its weavers, where is the loom?
If such is our society, what is to be spun?

◆

The republican revolution was the greatest utopian movement in
American history. The revolutionaries aimed at nothing less than a re-
constitution of American society. They hoped to destroy the bonds
holding together the older monarchical society—kinship, patriarchy,
and patronage—and to put in their place new social bonds of love, re-
spect, and consent.
      —Gordon S. Wood, *The Radicalism of the American Revolution*

◆

The United States was certainly, fundamentally, a federation, and a very
remarkable one of many parts, already expanding its membership and

programmed for further expansion. But that only emphasizes what an
uncertain creation it was: complex, asymmetrical, incomplete, unsta-
ble—and grandiose in scale and pretension.
                              —D.W. Meinig, *The Shaping of America: Volume I*

♦

To me, that sounds like a poem, like a blueprint
for the *Cantos* or *Paterson* or *Leaves of Grass,*
like the geography of a great novel, say *Moby Dick*
or *U.S.A.* It sounds like something worth reading,
assembling, grappling with, comprehending. Of course
it does. But how? How to encompass such
magnitude when even this single city block denies me?
How to decipher a map of Brobdignagian scale?
To understand America you must understand
its history and geology and sociopathologies,
its belts of rust and sun and grain. To understand America
you must understand its wealth and its poverty,
its greed, its generosity, its idealism, its isolation,
its myths, illusions, vices, hungers. You must understand
the formal beauty of a Shaker chair and Georgia
O'Keeffe's "Red Canna" and Bill Traylor's "Yellow Chicken"
and the light that inhabits both graveyard and mountains
in "Moonrise, Hernandez, New Mexico, 1941."
You must understand why Woody Guthrie sang
"Lonesome Road Blues" to a Scots-Irish melody
while riding the rails west from Oklahoma,
why Robert Johnson went down to the crossroads,
how "Sweet Home, Chicago" begets "Sweet Home, Alabama"
in a musical cartography that inverts the historical
geography of place with a racial transposition
that some would call cultural exploitation
and others a sign of the melting pot at full boil.
To understand America you must understand the vision
of William Byrd II rising early to study the Bible,
read from Ovid, and whip the slave girl Jenny
for behaving unmannerly. You must understand
the ingenuity of Grant's army before Vicksburg,
pyramids of limbs behind the field hospital at Shiloh,
the way Lee's men lay down their weapons
and drift away like ghosts after Appomattox,

small buds of men walking home, all spring,
through the green-fingered fields of Virginia and Carolina.
To understand America you must smell the odor
of ancient popcorn and suck upon a petrified Twizzler
within the sanctified precincts of the Music Box theater
where the sky machine frees the souls of mechanical clouds
and you must laugh as the crowd laughs
at the absurd fraternal violence of the Three Stooges film festival
and feel in that sheltered place a deep-rooted communion
that will last as long as the darkness lasts
and disperse with its members onto windy avenues
of particulate commerce and falling snow.
To understand America you must understand
the kinds of community we are and are not.
To understand America you must understand the dream.

♦

In 1642 a Huron man dreamed that non-Huron Iroquois had taken him
and burned him as a captive. As soon as he awoke, a council was held.
"The ill fortune of such a Dream," said the chiefs, "must be averted." At
once twelve or thirteen fires were lighted in the cabin where captives
were burned, and torturers seized firebrands. The dreamer was burned:
"he shrieked like a madman. When he avoided one fire, he at once fell
into another." Naked, he stumbled around the fires three times, singed
by one torch after another, while his friends repeated compassionately,
"courage, my Brother, it is thus that we have pity on thee."
　　　　　　　　　—Anthony F. C. Wallace, *The Death and Rebirth of the Seneca*

♦

Thus the sacred *Ondinnonk* of the Iroquois, "a secret desire of the soul
　　manifested by a dream."
Thus William Tecumseh Sherman, who spoke of battle as of a dream, hazy
　　and unreal,
the same feeling he knew painting landscapes at home in Ohio before the
　　war.
Thus my own father, son of an immigrant, for whom the American Dream
　　described a predictive trajectory,
a literal and symbolic enactment, though surely he, of all people, should
　　appreciate the significance of wish-fulfillment.

He is, after all, a psychoanalyst,

a head-shrinker, in popular dialect, referring, I guess, to the cannibal tribes
    of the Amazon or Vanuatu,
though I have always formulated an association with the Mold-A-Rama
    machine in the Museum of Science & Industry
that manufactures plastic statuettes of Abraham Lincoln for a dollar, pistons
    pulsing, heat meters rising,
the hiss of fluid steam-injected to the mold which pops apart to birth a still-
    hot waxy white souvenir into the slot.

Thus the deep-woven dreams of Melanesia,

omen of bats and kingfishers, oath-stones bound in spiderweb, odor of
    gardenias carried up from the jungle,
flowers in sunlight releasing their fragrance, their blood perfume—the
    same smell these tulips dying on the radiator give forth—
the smell of our wedding, of course, ritual rings and vows beneath a
    blossoming dogwood in a Baltimore backyard.

Three weeks later, we find ourselves climbing the volcanic cone of Mount
    Yasur at sunset,
wind warming to flame the jagged cinders on which we kneel to watch the
    pit belch forth black clouds of smoke and bile,
a rumbling pulse of tiny earthquakes, three per minute, and then the lava
    blooming upward like prayerful hands,
like brain coral or a red balloon seeking its outer limit of expansion,
    suspended, hesitant, collapsing against the far wall of the crater to cool,
black skin over molten flesh sliding back to the crucible as seals reentering
    water with the liquid suck and hiss of a belly wound,
plasma rich with oxygen seeping from an incision, vital organs hidden from
    view, the sibilance of molten rock and metal.

Picture that vista from the lip of the volcano back across the ash plain,
    across the sterile, sulphurous lake bed
to the mountains robed and hemmed in green, the jungled escarpment
    beyond which lies the rugged coast,
villages where the men believe an army burns within the three caldera
    percolating beneath us,
black soldiers, Americans, an Army of Spiritual Renewal, vengeful and
    nativist, anti-colonial, a millennial wave
come to sweep the white man off the syncretic rocks of local belief and into
    the ocean from whence he arose.

Picture the view all the way back across the ridges and valleys of the
    slumbering archipelago to July 16, 1774,
when Captain Cook first came across it, brooding like giant tortoises
    shawled in mist and vapors,
and proceeded to chart and survey with characteristic zeal, puzzling at the
    grim response of the ni-Vanuatu,
who met him with the studied indifference reserved for unwanted
    intruders from the kingdom of the ancestors.

On Malakula they failed to offer food,
nor would they barter for goods;

on Erromango they threw stones
and were answered with bullets.

So were established the terms of the dialogue.

                    ◆

So the centuries passed, and the ni-Vanuatu were colonized; white men
    came to live among them and enslave them to their god.
In time they sought to comprehend the sorcery of the white man's wealth,
    to decode his rituals and occult colonial vanities,
to master his symbolic magic with counterfeit flags and "customs
    documents" scrawled upon palm fronds,

but their bamboo radios could not receive the frequencies of the spirit
    world, nor did their jungle warehouses fill with food,
nor could their wooden planes, arrayed as a duck hunter deploys his decoys,
    lure the commodity gods from the sky,
nor did their mock currency stamped with the sign of a coconut unlock the
    imperious mystery of capital.

                    ◆

The whole explanatory scheme of the world brought by the whites and
their missionaries is so utterly alien to the traditional knowledge of the
natives that they are unable to grasp it. . . . For example, the natives re-
gard the fact that the white men cropped up from nowhere, and yet
seem very prosperous, as something in need of an explanation, just as we
might see the need for an explanation if numbers of people with wings
and harps and happy expressions suddenly descended and colonized us.
            —I.C. Jarvie, "Theories of Cargo Cults: A Critical Analysis"

The new cult endeavors to copy significant European activities. There is the belief in shipping, that is in the origin of cargoes—for remember that most Melanesians have not seen or experienced the manufacturing process. There is a mystical significance . . . in money, which circulates so strangely; in flags and flag-poles, which the European treats with peculiar reverence; . . . in soldiers and drilling—which must be mystical, for what use is there in it?

—Cyril Belshaw, *Changing Melanesia*

♦

Village census-books and the hats of government-appointed officials were now burned; people became seized with twitchings and saw visions; property was hurled into the sea, especially traditional objects and even the skulls of the dead so important in the ancestor cult; people claimed to have *seen* the Cargo ships unloading. Planes were coming; the ancestors were returning; and the docks were built for the Cargo vessels.

—Peter Worsley, *And the Trumpet Shall Sound*

♦

So it was, in 1942, that the U.S. Marines arrived to construct an advance
    base for the battle unfolding to the north—Guadalcanal—
and a city arose from the jungle, with coral roads built by the Seabees,
    Quonset huts to house a hundred thousand men,
sawmills and machine shops, dry docks, a radio station, a Masonic temple, a
    mammoth steam laundry,
four hospitals, five airfields, forty-three movie theaters showing Bob Hope
    in *My Favorite Blonde*.

How not to worship this miraculous manifestation!
How not to wonder at this world-creating system!

And then, just as suddenly, the war was over, and the Army sought to sell
    its surplus for a token sum to the local French colonial planters
who, expecting to get it for free, refused, and so to prove a point we built a
    jetty far out into the channel,
and rolled those improbable tons of ordinance into the sea, and ignited it all
    with underwater charges to prevent any usable salvage.

And even today America's wealth and profligacy remain manifest at
   Million Dollar Point, a strange syncresis of corrosion and growth,
a bizarre moonscape of sorrowful wreckage, the components of a hundred
   unidentifiable machines fused and transformed to an unearthly alloy,
crane derricks grown into the living reef, truck engines encompassed by
   polyps and rusted jeeps crusted with delicate anemones,
a cache of numberless nuts and bolts, bullets and cowrie shells, drifted
   coconut husks and fossilized eyedroppers,

and casting a familiar sheen across it all the unmistakable remains of tens of
   thousands of Coca-Cola bottles,
entire cases overgrown with sponges and fan coral, inhabited by tiny crabs
   and phosphorescent silver fish,
rings and lips, aqua necks, twisted torsos, innumerable shards rounded and
   polished
to every caliber of blue-green grit, irredeemable chits and tokens, brilliant
   pebbles in the tide wash.

◆

There are systems and there are systems.
There are systems within systems.

◆

There is no system!

◆

What used to be called the "Hollywood firmament" formed a system
entire unto itself, with its own variables, a human typology. The actors
represented models of character and behavior; there was a hero for
every temperament; for those who aimed to tackle life through action,
Clark Gable represented a sort of brutality leavened with boastful swag-
ger, Gary Cooper was cold blood filtered through irony; for those who
counted on overcoming obstacles with a mixture of humor and savoir
faire, there was the aplomb of William Powell and discretion of Fran-
chot Tone; for the introvert who masters his shyness there was James
Stewart, while Spencer Tracy was the model of the just, open-minded
man who knows how to do things with his hands; and we were given a
rare example of the intellectual hero in Leslie Howard.
                              —Italo Calvino, "A Cinema-Goer's Autobiography"

And what about Bob Hope?

To which type, which model, which identity does he conform?

What human truth does he embody?

What are we to make of him, and of ourselves, in whose image he has been
     made?

Bob the everyman, Bob the plutocrat, Bob the comic coward, Bob the
     soldier's pal.

Bob the chicken, Bob the hawk, Bob the letch, Bob the shill.

Bob the pitchman, Bob the pennypinch, Bob the paradigm, Bob the
     paradox.

Even as a kid I never understood him, Bob "for Big Money" Hope,
     proferring something corporate and not of my world,

and his swank Christmas specials in celebration of celebrity, and the
     anachronistic movies that would appear on weekend afternoons,

*Son of Paleface, Call Me Bwana, I'll Take Sweden,* how they failed to signify
     after John Wayne or Tarzan or even Godzilla,

a more ironic archetype, riddled with ambiguity, the understanding of
     which even now entraps and eludes me,

though I feel I must find my way toward some resolution, because it is my
     obligation to carry him with me,

to explicate and account for him as I was tutored in a vision of the culture
     embodied and passed down through iconographic ritual and myth,

as I remember a particular longago Saturday when my father called me
     home from the crabgrass and swing sets

to watch with him the Marx Brothers on our black-and-white TV, my
     introduction to the zeitgeist and the language that would claim me,

the razzledazzle of the multicultural demotic,

the sacred vernacular of the absurd,

and I like to think it was neither *Duck Soup* nor *A Night at the Opera* but
     *The Big Store* that we watched,

thereby not merely an exercise in the material comedy of human
     consumption but an object lesson in loss,

a sadly inferior film, proof of the inevitability of our decline, which would
     explain so much, I like to believe,

though in truth this whole episode feels too shadowless a fantasy or screen,
    a collage contrived from stolen fragments,
and yet, for all its artifice, for all it may be a dream, I hunger no less for the
    manna that it offers.

♦

Go on, believe! It does no harm.

—Wittgenstein, *Culture and Value*

♦

The system revolves around faith; the invisible
hand annoints, the iron cage opens and closes reluctantly;
power corrupts; space warps and fractures; money
equals time; competition begets selective adaptation;
the taproot of language descends into the abyss
and the food chain unto the kingdom of the protozoa;
what's flesh is flesh and what's bone bone
and what sings in the blood is the bird of our being,
bird of paradise and bird of the ascent,
thousand-feathered bird of the blind will to power;
gravity's harp, the bells of desire, certain music never varies;
mandolins for the Irish, drums for the Yoruba,
the song is the same, whatever its tempo or instrumentation,
the flotsam and jetsam of historical circumstance,
glyphs in a sea of amniotic fluid, bright figures
reflected in the wake of our passage
as the waves and urges that bind and drive us,
compared to which the cartoon gods are merciful
in their cruelty, technicolor death held suspended
like the tantalizing anvils of Wile E. Coyote,
deadly but incorporeal, freighted with the blur-significance
of dreams. The system revolves around dreams
like a honky-tonk carousel, instead of wooden horses
the ghosts of dead Presidents resurrected by Disney,
pulse and swell of commercial jingles
from the steam calliope because the key is epic,
because we have so little history of our own
and what there is beneath the meadows of Queen Anne's lace
is not so much the colorful words or uniforms
but a noise like a woman tearing burlap into rags,

the roar of guns in a distant valley or the ocean
against a well-constructed barrier of riprap,
the tide's erosion of what remains concrete: America
as a nation of dreams; their birth; their realization
or failure to be realized; their ignominious death.
The system revolves around death: regicide, suicide,
stillicide; the inalienable right to explode into fragments;
the right to sing oneself at the expense of all others;
the right to gravitate earthward; the right to draw back
into the whirling anonymity of the storm. The system
revolves around myth: snowflake motifs of local belief
spray-painted on empty department store windows,
ritual dreams forever reenacted within the cinema
of the psyche, silent films projected upon the heavens
like a filigreed cosmology or a Map of the Stars,
quasars and pulsars or Scorpio and Cygnus,
the imponderable Milky Way or the streets of Beverly Hills,
the one a mere reflection of the other's glory,
as any model provides a means of repudiating entropy,
Scorpion or Swan, Hollywood or double helix,
still lifes, nature studies, formal gardens, foreign currency,
fountains to give meaning to the movement of water,
to comfort those who would consider the cascade.
And while there are no constellations named *Bob Hope,*
*Lady Liberty, Sutter's Mill, The White City,*
it is our birthright to bear these crosses
and albatrosses forward, to seek meaning in their fire,
to define the intrinsic patterns of their panoply
and invest them with reflected illumination,
as any movie lends some vision of formal coherence
to the wall's blank canvas, as the green light
is rendered tragic by the pathos of Gatsby's obsession,
as the stars are merely stars until we order them
in ranks and columns, fifty states and thirteen stripes,
one nation, indivisible. The system revolves
around order; the system revolves around chaos.
The system revolves around community; the system
revolves around the individual. To understand
America, you must first understand the system.

# VI

## Hope: An Elegy

*Tomorrow at the latest I'll start working on a great book*
*In which my century will appear as it really was.*
                                    —*Czeslaw Milosz*

At last the snow begins to slow its glum descent, as well it should, wound
    down to flurries and idle worries,
a weary diminuendo of unsyncopated flakes and solitary trajectories, the
    city's sacrificial interment complete,
sent across as on some Pharoanic funerary barge replete with vestal retinue
    and commodious store of goods,
leaving in its wake a world immaculate and polished as a waxed-up apple
    or neonate or Chevy,

a brand new Chicago cast in ersatz crystal.

I guess George Kennedy can scrape the runway free of ice at last, Dean
    Martin bring the plane down for an emergency landing
in which it shall be revealed that his stewardess-mistress Jackie Bisset has
    lost the baby she was secretly bearing,
while Maureen Stapleton haunts the concourse begging forgiveness for her
    husband the hated and unhinged bomber,

though right now, old Dino should be winging his way across less familiar
    skies, sipping martinis in alien isolation,
scanning the horizon for sign of his final destination, that last cocktail
    lounge engagement in the world beyond.

Taps.
Solitude and darkness.
Day is done,

and what, in the end, can I offer up as proof of its passage?

Hollywood did not beat down my door.
I failed to complete the next installment of my Elvis screen trilogy.
I have discovered no uncharted island
nor is my catalogue *raisonné* complete,
nor did I perform sit-ups to combat winter fat,

reduce my dependence on foreign oil,
or invest for the college education of future generations.

Tomorrow.
OK?

Tomorrow.

◆

Today, the time has come to confront the grim actuality of the snow, the
      onus of this elemental, heaven-forgéd stuff,
the weight of excavation, the work of removal, with the steps icing over
      already, Elizabeth due so soon,
though it looks incredibly cold out there, sheer agony to assume when my
      tea is still warm, when I can turn up the music for a moment
and dance euphorically around the apartment to the beat of something
      monumentally undemanding.

And even if I admit this happiness to be the by-product of caffeine and
      adrenaline and a dance-induced release of endorphins,
and even if this music antagonizes the neighbors, and my wool socks stick
      and fray against the splintering floor,
I tell you it has been ratified by the belly kicks of the unborn, and not for all
      the golf balls in Palm Springs would I trade this humble joy.

◆

O how I wonder
where that old snow shovel
is!

◆

*After Issa*

   Writing shit about new snow
for the rich
   is not art; but then,

writing shit about new snow
   for the sake of art
is not enriching.

♦

Look now—joggers!
In this snow! Serious sickness,
    or just fucked up?


♦


When I jog along the lake these days, or when we walk that path to visit the
    great apes at the Lincoln Park Zoo,
finding in their tenderness and familial roughhousing a sympathetic vision
    of that which awaits us,
I no longer pass the statue of steadfast Linnaeus but a marble bust of
    Emanuel Swedenborg ringed by sugar maples,
an odd couple of illustrious Swedes erected by what unfathomable cohort of
    Scandinavian intelligentsia.

So the arch-rationalist
is replaced by the mystic.

Is this some kind of parable?


♦


The origin of the species is the origin of the invisible, isolating walls that
arise between two populations and make them living islands.
                                —Jonathan Weiner, *The Beak of the Finch*


♦


Home from the voyage of the *Beagle,* Darwin invested the next seven years
    in the study and taxonomy of barnacles,
mapping their divergence, cataloguing by family and genus, seeking the
    invisible hand behind their multiplicity and variation.

After the birth of his children, he studied the chimpanzees at the London
    zoo, pondering the heritability of emotions,
contemplating the instinctive responses of fear, surprise, laughter,
    comparing their expressions with those of his son back home in Down,
identifying at last the fatal mechanism of natural selection only after
    reading Malthus' *On Population.*

Following years of stability the wild chimpanzees under study by Jane
    Goodall peacefully separated into two distinct clans;
in the long months thereafter the larger group systematically annihilated
    the smaller:
females and children were forcibly reincorporated into the vestigial tribe;
    the males were hunted down

and killed, one by one, in the forest.

So must the Hawaiians have stood, at Kealakekua Bay, Cook's body in the
    surf before them, his blood upon their hands,
and wondered, looking up, at the consequences of their actions, and the
    terrible vengeance such a god would wreak on his return.


◆


We with our lives are like islands in the sea, or like trees in the forest.
The maple and the pine may whisper to each other with their leaves,
and Conanicut and Newport hear each other's foghorns. But the trees
also commingle their roots in the darkness underground, and the is-
lands also hang together through the ocean's bottom.
                                    —William James, *On Psychical Research*


◆


If no man is an island, who's to say an island is?

Seen from underwater, Hawaii is not disjunct but continuous, a sequence of
    ripples in the skin of the orange.
Any peak or atoll or rocky shoal can be classified as part of some larger
    system if the scale on the map remains fluid,
as the earth is a cog in the solar archipelago, the sun a snowflake in the
    blizzard of the galaxy.

But even if there were a scale that could accommodate this storm, what
    good is any chart on a journey propelled by unfathomable currents?
Are we doomed to repeat the errors of past voyages: Columbus and the
    Arawaks, Cook's fatal search for the "Northwest Passage"?
Is it ever possible to distinguish the myths of yesterday from the reality of
    this moment from the dream of what is yet to come?
Can we truly hope to seal the leaks in our keel? Is there yet some unknown
    land to save us from the flood?

What of lost Atlantis, the fabled continents of Lemuria and Mu? Why
   won't the Air Force release the photographs of Hangar 51?

Hangar 12. Hangar 17.
Whatever.

Imagine the ocean of loneliness when we stand alone in a world of our
   absolute making.
Imagine how we'll mourn what we so heedlessly destroy.
Imagine the hunger for solid earth beneath our feet when at last we set sail
   upon that limitless sea.

◆

Saddest of all is the Kauai *o'o* . . . In the early 1890s the birds were com-
mon and the forest was filled with their beautiful song. By 1973 a mere
forty birds survived. Now in the mornings in the Alakai Swamp, a sin-
gle, haunting and persistent call is occasionally heard. It belongs to one
lonely male, the last of the *o'o*s, who sings each day for a mate. He sings
a requiem for his species, for no female now exists.
                              —Andrew Mitchell, *The Fragile South Pacific*

◆

The formation of different languages and of distinct species, and the
proofs that both have been developed through a gradual process, are cu-
riously parallel . . . Dominant languages and dialects spread widely, and
lead to the gradual extinction of other tongues. A language, like a
species, when extinct, never . . . reappears.
                              —Darwin, *The Descent of Man*

◆

Only about 600 languages are reasonably safe by dint of the sheer num-
ber of their speakers . . . and this optimistic assumption still suggests
that between 3,600 and 5,400 languages, as many as 90% of the world's
total, are threatened with extinction in the next century.
                              —Stephen Pinker, *The Language Instinct*

◆

At a facility outside Atlanta, research apes no longer needed for experi-
mentation spend their days gesturing in the sign language they have

faithfully mastered to keepers unable to understand them.

—National Geographic

◆

*The limits of my language* mean the limits of my world.

—Wittgenstein, Tractatus

◆

And beyond those limits, what would we discover:
dragons, antimatter, the holy, the irrational?
And what vessel should we employ to visit that realm:
vision quest, Chaos Theory, suicide, glossolalia?

Whatever's there, it is real and it is unknowable.
By any form of transit, we shall never reach that shore.

Our structures of comprehension do not encompass it.
Our grammar can not render it.
Our engines will not burn that element.

It takes a mighty effort of will to disavow the demons
in the corners of the cathedral, and even then,
what certainty has our fearful rigor engendered?
Are we to kill again that familiar figure
when the headless torso rises animate from the table?

With what would we bargain for immunity from prosecution?
Where would we seek sanctuary?
And the cost of the journey?
And the names of the shadows inscribed on the map?

How are we to contemplate that fantastic voyage now, earthbound and ill-
    prepared?

Like flightless birds we have evolved imperfectly
downward from the celestial.

At night we dream of reckless soaring;
our hollow bones still ring with wind.

Would you believe it, if I told you, that even now, as I write these lines, as I
  dance this little caffeine-buzz shuffle,
word comes over the radio that Bob Hope has passed over to the great
  beyond, gone to fetch his eternal reward,
retired at last to vaudeville Valhalla, that heavenly Pro-Am, that never-
  ending celebrity roast in the sky?

What matter if it's true, if it is inevitable?
If not today, tomorrow; if not tomorrow, yesterday.
Who among us can predict the future?

For that matter, who can predict the past,
except to say that this, too, shall surely pass,
that death is nothing if not absolute?

Already I see his picture
on the cover
of *People* magazine,

young and beautiful Bob, smiling his smile of purest mastery, leering the
  leer of an era untroubled by doubt or uncertainty.

Bob agog with Bing on the golf course, Bob playing kissy with second-
  string starlets.
Bob pushing Pepsodent, Bob shopping Oscars, Bob selling war bonds with
  Eleanor Roosevelt.
Bob in the jungles of Guadalcanal, Bob raising the flag on Iwo Jima, Bob as
  Coyote, Bob as Loki, Bob in the ashes of Nagasaki.
Bob as Cook, Bob as Darwin, Bob as Columbus, Bob as Buzz Aldrin.
Bob in Palm Springs with the ghosts of dead Presidents, Bob in bronze at
  the Museum of American History, Bob teeing off in the Sea of Serenity.
Bob the body and Bob the shadow, Bob the echo and Bob the call.
Bob the imperial envoy of the American System, Bob the corporate
  janissary, Bob the mad jester of cultural hegemony.

THANKS FOR THE MEMORY!

So long. Farewell. Good-bye,
sweet Bob.
Adios, adieu, aloha.

Sayonara,
as Bing would say.

Sayonara on a steel guitar.

♦

> For as this appalling ocean surrounds the verdant land, so in the soul of
> man there lies an insular Tahiti, full of peace and joy, but encompassed
> by all the horrors of the half known life. God keep thee! Push not off
> from that isle, thou canst never return!
>
> —Melville, *Moby Dick*

♦

I see the squirrels have closed up shop for the night, nest sealed tight against
    the cold, though we're sure to enjoy their company again
come dawn, scavenging seeds from the neighbor's plastic bird feeder,
    digging and hoarding to last until spring,
when yet another crop will poke their quizzical, finger-puppet heads from
    the nest to confront their arboreal destiny.

How I envy them their hunting-and-gathering, bringing home the bacon,
    the sunflower seeds, the bread crusts,
while I lie sleepless and sweat-soaked at night, eaten by worries, consumed
    by the bottomless fear of the provider.

What chutzpah, to birth an annual brood, to loose another generation in the
    treetops, to toss those fuzzy ontological dice,
the creative will of the body, against which a poem or a language or a model
    of discourse is as a mote in heaven's eye,
all of our immaculate systems and constructs repudiated by a squirrel, an
    elm tree, a snow storm, an embryo,
the mortal weight of the power to bring another being into this world of
    happiness pursued and unpursued,

this world of ravening sorrow,
this world of the beauty and fragility of falling snow.

No, I cannot bring myself to share the faith in that unmitigated paradise the
    landlord so regularly broadcasts,
though I admit the suburbs are a complex theme, the forest preserve
    unknown to me, much about Chicagoland still shrouded in mystery.

What our landlord doesn't know is that I've hidden his squirrel trap
    beneath the gardening tools on the landing,
because I no longer have the will to implicate myself in their suffering, I am
    content to bear their idiot scratchings,
I don't even feel guilty about it anymore, the minor damage they do to his
    walls, the leaks, the holes, the pilfered insulation,
not even the leftover Thanksgiving walnuts Elizabeth has cast by the
    dozens beneath their ancient elm.

&#9830;

Then the qualities, almost emotional, palpably artistic, heroic, of a tree;
so innocent and harmless, yet so savage. It *is,* yet says nothing. How it re-
bukes by its tough and equable serenity all weathers, this gusty-tem-
per'd little whiffet, man, that runs indoors at a mite of rain or snow.

—Whitman, Specimen Days

&#9830;

It is in midwinter that I sometimes glean from my pines something
more important than woodlot politics, and the news of the wind and
weather. This is especially likely to happen on some gloomy evening
when the snow has buried all irrelevant detail, and the hush of elemen-
tal sadness lies heavy upon every living thing. Nevertheless, my pines,
each with his burden of snow, are standing ramrod-straight, rank upon
rank, and in the dusk beyond I sense the presence of hundreds more. At
such times I feel a curious transfusion of courage.

—Aldo Leopold, Sand County Almanac

&#9830;

And now at last I'm digging among the hill shapes and divots, drumlins
    and eskers, glacial metaphors deposited like gravel.
I'm plowing the runway, I'm building a reef, I'm prospecting for gold, I'm
    rowing for the promise of a distant shore.
I'm working like a machine, ribs beneath flesh, beneath the sheared hair of
    Irish sheep, beneath a skin of space-age polymer.

Behold, my old
snow shovel!
I grasp it in my hand

like an oar.

Like an axe.
Like a sword, like a staff,
like a sign.

True, I could borrow the landlord's sack of salt and toxic particles from
     behind the washing machine in the basement,
sow those lethal crystals to battle the beautiful army of ice, but my heart just
     isn't into chemical warfare.

From here, my window looks small and golden, nostalgic, honey-fed; it
     glows the way childhood glows, irretrievable.

From Clark Street comes the glimmer-dance of traffic,
blind eyes of the high-rise,
dim rumble of the El in the distance.

With any luck, I'll be finished in time to meet Elizabeth at the train, walk
     her home, attend to the business of stoking the furnace.


     ♦

Let's see now, mu-shu
and egg rolls
from Ho Wah Garden,

or deep-dish sausage-
stuffed
Chicago-style pizza?


     ♦


Tomorrow, with any luck, this snow
will be forgotten, plowed into the margins,
consigned to pockets and corners of shade.

The sun could come out.
It might warm up a few degrees.
A kind of palest blue could film the sky.

With any luck, no more than tartan stripes of frost
will remain to contest with in the morning,
city pavement salt-licked and ice-glossed

with borrowed ingots and unpayable notes,
spots of slick glitter like numberless coins
forged in the mint of bodies and hours.

Another day,
another dollar!

Scalloped and haloed, arched and buttressed by the silent branches of the
      elm, a world of undulant shadow surrounds me,
a world of ice against which I struggle to carve a human foothold,
a world predestined for oblivion and loss, a world alive with the promise of
      transformation and renewal.

My ears throb.
My hands are numb already.
My body cries out against the cold.

&#9670;

*Courage, my brother, it is thus that we have pity on thee.*

*Let us fight for the flagpole alone.*

&#9670;

*This is a kind of thing that happens.*

&#9670;

Hope springs eternal.

# PART 3

# PREGNANCY TRIPTYCH

This morning we find dead earthworms in the dining room again.

Yesterday there were three; the day before one,

solitary traveller, lone pilgrim or pioneer shrivelled up hard and black as the
twist-tie I first mistook it for, shrunken and bloodless, brittle as wire.

Today it's two, a couple, bodies entwined in a death-embrace

become a cryptic glyph or sign, some Masonic rune or Buddhist talisman
glimpsed in a Chinatown junk shop—

the ideogram of this mysterious manifestation.

*So shall they come amongst us, singly and by pairs.*

But where have they come from? The ficus? The yucca? A paltry,
crumbled trail of soil implicates the rubber tree, solemn in its dusty corner,
in its green wicker basket among bookshelves. Is it possible? After all these
years, how could it contain so much primordial, undomesticated life, so
many wandering waves of worms? And what would induce them to leave it
now, that safe haven of roots and humus, to migrate out into the great wide
world, to wither and die in the vast dilapidated Sahara of our dining room
floor?

Inseparable love? Biological compulsion? The change

of seasons? Autumn. Former students call

to speak of their suicides; the last yellow jackets

dive like enraged kamikazes to die enmeshed in our window screens,
rusted auto-bodies awaiting the wrecker;

higher up, two geese,

vectored west against the contrails from O'Hare.

Last week two squirrels burst into my sister-in-law Becky's apartment and
ran amok in a leaf-storm of old mail and newspapers, chewing through a

blueberry muffin and a box of Frango mints, whirling like the waters of the southern hemisphere counterclockwise around the living room until she chased them with a broom back out the open window.

From my window I watch the local squirrels settling in for the season, hoarding burrs and acorns and catkins, feathering their nest in the hollow limb of the big elm tree with insulation stolen by the mouthful from our attic.

At the church next door kids released early from evening service toss ping pong balls into colored buckets;

chimney swallows emerge from the unused smokestack that marks its former existence as a carriage factory to scour the dusk for insects, scattering and coalescing in fugitive rings,

coming together, breaking apart, coming together, breaking apart,

circling and circling in a sinuous wreath, ecstatic ash from the soul's bright burning.

Dusk: bicyclists; cricket chimes; the blue moon;

a single green planetary orb to grace the withered stalks of the tomato plants

in the garden. In the kitchen,

after removing the oatmeal raisin cookies to cool, Elizabeth has fallen asleep in the flour-dusted afterglow of baking,

in the sluice of pooled heat spilled like sugared lava from the oven,

in her clothes, on the floor,

sitting up.

is where we turned around, surrendered to fate, gave in to defeat and abandoned our journey at a town with three stoplights, one good mechanic and a name of possibly oracular significance.

Which is how we came to consider calling the baby Delphos.

Which is why we never made it to Pennsylvania, never arrived to help J.B. plant trees on the naked mountaintop he calls a farm, never hiked down the brush-choked trail for groceries in the gnomic hamlet of Mann's Choice, never hefted those truckloads of bundled bodies nor buried their delicate rootling toes in the ice and mud of rocky meadows.

Blue spruce, black walnut, white pine, silver maple.

And that name! Mann's Choice. Finger of individual will poked in the face of inexorable destiny.

Which is how we came to consider calling the baby Hamlet, Spruce or Pennsylvania.

But we didn't make it there. Never even got to Lima or Bucyrus, let alone Martin's Ferry, let alone West Virginia, let alone the Alleghenies tumbled across the state line like the worn-out molars of a broken-down plow horse munching grass in a hayfield along the slate grey Juniata.

Because the engine balked.

Because the shakes kicked in and grew like cornstalks hard as we tried to ignore them, as if we could push that battered blue Volvo across the wintry heart of the Midwest through sheer determination.

Which is foolish.

And the man in Delphos told us so.

Fuel injector, he says. Can't find even a sparkplug for foreign cars in these parts. Nearest dealer would be Toledo or Columbus, or down the road in Fort Wayne.

Which is Indiana. Which is going backwards.

Which is why they drive Fords in Ohio.

Which is how we came to consider calling the baby Edsel, Henry, Pinto or Sparks.

Which is why we spent the last short hour of evening lurching and vibrating back through those prosperous bean fields just waiting for spring to burst the green-shingled barns of Van Wert County.

Which is how we came to consider calling the baby Verna, Daisy, Persephone or Soy.

By this time we're back on the freeway, bypassing beautiful downtown Fort Wayne in favor of the rain forest at Exit 11, such is the cognomen of this illuminated Babel, this litany, this sculptural aviary for neon birds, these towering aluminum and tungsten weeds,

bright names raised up like burning irons to brand their sign upon the heavens.

Exxon, Burger King, Budgetel, Super 8.

Which is how we came to consider calling the baby Bob Evans.

Which is how we came to consider calling the baby Big Boy, Wendy, Long John Silver or Starvin' Marvin.

Which is how we came to salve our wounds by choosing a slightly better than average motel, and bringing in the Colonel to watch "Barnaby Jones" while Elizabeth passes out quick as you like

leaving me alone with my thoughts and reruns

in the oversized bed of an antiseptic room on an anonymous strip of indistinguishable modules among the unzoned outskirts of a small midwestern city named for the Indian killer Mad Anthony Wayne.

Which is why I'm awake at 4 a.m. as the first trucks sheet their thunder down toward the interstate.

Which is when I feel my unborn child kick and roll within the belly of its sleeping mother, three heartbeats in two bodies, two bodies in one blanket, one perfect and inviolable will like a flower preparing to burst into bloom,

and its aurora lights the edge of the window like nothing I've ever seen.

All through those final, fitful weeks we walked off the restlessness of our daily expectancy on the avenues of sun-hunger and recalcitrant slush.

When would that big fat beautiful baby

blue first day of spring arrive?

So we strolled the backstreets and boulevards to consider the clouds and drink some decaf and escape the press of solicitous voices, gingerly, leaving feathers unruffled, like that first, fearless pair of mallards coasting the lake's archipelagoes of melting ice. We walked to the movies, again and again— Eddie Murphy at the Biograph, Orson Welles amid the Moorish splendor of the Music Box—varying our route until we knew every block in the neighborhood, every greystone and three-flat, every Sensei sushi bar and Michoaqueno flower stall.

We walked to Ho Wah Garden and the Ostoneria and over to Becky's for deep-dish pizza;

to Manny's for waffles on mornings of aluminum rain;

the German butcher for bratwurst, the Greek bakery for elephant ears, the 7-11 for cocktail onions to satisfy Elizabeth's idiosyncratic cravings.

We walked until our fears resurfaced and then we ate our fears.

We walked ourselves right out of winter into precincts we knew and those we didn't and some the city kept as private enclaves for itself, a certain statue, a street of saris, an oasis of cobbled lanes amid the welter of industry where suddenly the forsythia is in lightning-fierce flower, sudden as lilac, as bells, as thunder rolling in from the plains, sky a bruised melon spawning ocean-green hailstones to carry our rusted storm gutters away in an avalanche of kerneled ice plastered with bankrolls of last year's leaves.

Behold the daffodil, behold the crocus!

Behold the awakened, the reborn, the already onrushing furious and blooming:

violets overgrown in the lawn gone back to prairie,

some trumpet-flowered vine exuding sweet ichor upon the vacant house across the street,

dandelions blown to seed

and the ancient Japanese widows who stoop to gather their vinegar-bitter stems.

That final morning we clear the cobwebs and crack the storm windows to let the breeze take shelter in our closets and to bask all day in its muddy, immutable odor. Elizabeth naps in a chair by the window, attuned to the ring of a distant carrillon, matins and lauds, while down the block an unnumbered hoard of rollerblades and bicycles propel their passengers like locusts assembled at the toll of some physiological clock, the ancient correlation of sap and sunlight, equinoctial sugar and blood. The big elm has begun its slow adumbration of fluted leaflets and buds on branch tips, percussive nubs and fine-veined tympani, a many-fingered symphony tuning up.

Vespers: swallows and doves;

Elizabeth takes a final stitch in her tiny welcome blanket; yawns; done.

Bodies and hours, bodies and hours.

At midnight I close the book on final grades to find my desk alive with a host of translucent, freshly-fledged spiders, a microscopic multitude borne in on the breeze to take up residence among the computer keys, a vision that bears me down the umbilicus of dreams toward a dim, persistent, unreasoning rhythm, a music long promised, a visitation at last given up and unlooked for, ghostly silk loomed from winter's cocoon or the opening of one wind-shaken blossom——

*Behold the sleepers! When they wake everything,*

*o everything*

*shall be transformed.*

# ABOUT THE AUTHOR

CAMPBELL MCGRATH's other collections are *Capitalism, American Noise, Road Atlas* and *Florida Poems*. His awards include the Kingsley Tufts Prize, and fellowships from the Guggenheim and MacArthur Foundations. He teaches in the Creative Writing Program at Florida International University in Miami.